The Court of First Instance
of the European Communities

The Court of First Instance of the European Communities

Timothy Millett, M.A. (Oxon.)
of Gray's Inn, Barrister
Principal Administrator at the Court of Justice
of the European Communities

Butterworths
London, Edinburgh
1990

United Kingdom	Butterworth & Co (Publishers) Ltd, 88 Kingsway, LONDON WC2B 6AB and 4 Hill Street, EDINBURGH EH2 3JZ
Australia	Butterworths Pty Ltd, SYDNEY, MELBOURNE, BRISBANE, ADELAIDE, PERTH, CANBERRA and HOBART
Canada	Butterworths Canada Ltd, TORONTO and VANCOUVER
Ireland	Butterworth (Ireland) Ltd, DUBLIN
Malaysia	Malayan Law Journal Sdn Bhd, KUALA LUMPUR
New Zealand	Butterworths of New Zealand Ltd, WELLINGTON and AUCKLAND
Puerto Rico	Equity de Puerto Rico, Inc, HATO REY
Singapore	Malayan Law Journal Pte Ltd, SINGAPORE
USA	Butterworth Legal Publishers, AUSTIN, Texas; BOSTON, Massachusetts; CLEARWATER, Florida (D & S Publishers); ORFORD, New Hampshire (Equity Publishing); ST PAUL, Minnesota; and SEATTLE, Washington

A CIP Catalogue record for this book is available from the British Library.

ISBN 0 406 20222 2

Typeset by Phoenix Photosetting, Chatham, Kent
Printed and bound in Great Britain by Mackays of Chatham PLC, Chatham, Kent

Foreword

by Sir Gordon Slynn, Judge at the Court of Justice of the European Communities

There are probably few subjects on which Members of the European Court of Justice have been asked to give more lectures or to write more articles in recent months than on the new Court of First Instance which is now attached to the European Court of Justice and which has begun to hear cases. Amongst lawyers much interest has been aroused in this new Court – what cases go to it rather than to the European Court of Justice, how they begin, what are the procedures to be followed, what are the rights of appeal? For that reason it is splendid that the author and the publishers should have been able to produce this book so quickly.

It gives a useful and concise account of the reasons which led to the creation of the new Court of First Instance and of the considerations which had to be balanced as to what should be its jurisdiction, how it should be composed, to what extent its decisions should be subject to review by the European Court of Justice. Conversely, in the closing chapters, the author considers some of the problems which may still need to be resolved – should the jurisdiction of the Court of First Instance be extended; will one 'CFI' with the existing Court be enough to deal with the likely, perhaps inevitable, increase in cases before the European Court of Justice; what will be the real participation of the Advocate General; how can fact-finding be changed or improved; what will be the effect of the European Court's rulings on the points of law in one case on other cases which come later before the CFI (ie will the CFI be free to ignore or depart from the European Court's rulings other than in the case in question, when national courts applying Community law are expected or bound to follow them?) These are questions of interest to the development of the jurisdiction of the European Court and the Court of First Instance.

For the practitioner, however, this book has a more immediate value, since many cases – staff, competition, coal and steel – will have to be continued (from their commencement in the European Court of Justice) or begun before the new Court. The author explains clearly

and directly the procedures now to be applied before the new Rules of
Procedure (to be agreed by the Court and needing the unanimous
approval of the Council) are adopted. He brings together the provisions of the Treaty, the Decision establishing the Court of First
Instance, the Statutes of the Court of Justice and the Court of Justice's
Rules of Procedure to show how cases are to be commenced, and what
are the steps to be followed at each stage of the case.

Many of these steps are laid down in the European Court's Rules of
Procedure. Since, however, these are to be applied '*mutatis mutandis*',
it is valuable for the practitioner, particularly one not a regular at the
European Court, to have the views of this experienced author as to
how these rules are likely to be applied. It seems to me that the
chapters setting out the procedural steps give a very useful checklist of
what can be and what has to be done. There are in addition specific
sections dealing with interim relief, the extent to which related
damages claims can be dealt with and costs. The section on appeals
gives the most scope for forecasting, since obviously there is nothing in
the European Court's original Rules of Procedure dealing with them
and it contains useful guidance as to what is likely to be the procedure
followed by the Court of Justice.

What the new Rules of Procedure for the Court of First Instance will
provide, what the European Court of Justice and the Court of First
Instance will do in practice, remains to be seen (so that a second edition of this book will in due course be essential) but as a guide for the
present it is in my view timely and valuable.

January 1990

Preface

The establishment of the new Court of First Instance of the European Communities is a major event in the history of Community Law. The aim of this book is to give a complete and straightforward account of the new court and the system of appeals from it to the Court of Justice of the European Communities.

When it came to finding a short way of referring to each of the two courts, the natural choice – 'Court' – was excluded because it was ambiguous. Of the possible alternatives, I have chosen to refer to the 'ECJ' and the 'CFI' because those terms were at the same time brief and unambiguous.

Another question which arose was whether it was premature to write this book before the CFI had adopted its Rules of Procedure. In fact, the main outline of the CFI's procedure is already in place in the shape of Title III of the Statute, but the decisive factor was that the CFI itself was not prevented by the absence of its own Rules of Procedure from starting operations immediately. It is already dealing with a substantial number of cases transferred from the ECJ, applying the Rules of Procedure of the ECJ *mutatis mutandis*. Since the CFI is in operation, it seemed worthwhile to write this book describing the position as it now stands. I have endeavoured to state the law as at 1 November 1989.

As I am an official of the ECJ, I have to make it clear that the opinions expressed in this book do not reflect the position of the institution but are my personal views.

I am happy to express my gratitude to all those who have helped me produce this book. In particular I should like to thank Peter Rodney formerly of the Lord Chancellor's Department for his useful insights into the legislative texts, Denise Louterman of the ECJ's Registry for her help with the statistics, and Mrs Alison Dourdil-Diniz, Mrs Gill Gray and Mrs Linda Wynne-Williams for typing the manuscript. I should like to acknowledge my indebtedness to Sir Gordon Slynn and Francis Jacobs for whom I have worked as Legal Secretary at the ECJ for all that I have learned in working with them. Finally, I should like to express my deep appreciation to my wife Michèle for her support and encouragement in writing the book, which I dedicate to her.

Timothy Millett
5 December 1989

Contents

Abbreviations

CFI	Court of First Instance of the European Communities
ECJ	Court of Justice of the European Communities
ECSC	European Coal and Steel Community
ECSC Statute	Protocol on the Statute of the Court of Justice of the European Coal and Steel Community
EEC	European Economic Community
EEC Statute	Protocol on the Statute of the Court of Justice of the European Economic Community
Euratom	European Atomic Energy Community
Euratom Statute	Protocol on the Statute of the Court of Justice of the European Atomic Energy Community
OJ	Official Journal of the European Communities
The Decision	Council Decision 88/591/ECSC, EEC, Euratom of 24 October 1988 establishing a Court of First Instance of the European Communities (OJ 1988 L 319, p 1; corrected version OJ 1989 C 215, p 1)
The Statute	The EEC Statute. To simplify presentation, reference is made to the provisions of this Statute alone as including the corresponding provisions of the ECSC and Euratom Statutes, unless the context requires otherwise.
The Treaty	The EEC Treaty. To simplify presentation reference is made to the provisions of this Treaty alone as including the corresponding provisions of the ECSC and Euratom Treaties, unless the context requires otherwise.

Table of European Communities legislation

Secondary legislation

Conventions

Table of cases

Decisions of the European Court of Justice are listed both alphabetically and numerically. The numerical Table follows the alphabetical.

Decisions of the European Court of Justice are listed below numerically. These decisions are also included in the preceding alphabetical Table.

1   The establishment of the CFI

Historical background

As can be seen from the figures in Table I, the number of cases brought before the ECJ has steadily risen over the years, from 79 in 1970 to an average approaching 400 in the late 1980's. The ECJ has delivered more judgments, passing from 64 in 1970 to 208 in 1987 and 238 in 1988. Not all cases reach the stage of a final judgment: for instance, some are withdrawn and others are dismissed as inadmissible by reasoned order. A substantial number of cases are also joined, which allows several cases to be disposed of by a single judgment. Thus the total number of cases disposed of is approximately half as many again as the number of final judgments delivered. Nevertheless, the ECJ's capacity to dispose of cases has not kept pace with the increase in the number of cases brought before it. This is reflected particularly in the number of cases left pending before the ECJ, which has steadily grown, from 328 at the end of 1980 to an impressive 605 at the end of 1988. The result has been a marked lengthening in the average duration of proceedings before the ECJ. In 1975 the average length of time needed to obtain a preliminary ruling was six months; in 1980 it was nine months; and in 1988 it had reached 18 months. Likewise, the average length of time needed to obtain judgment in a direct action has risen from nine months in 1975 to 18 months in 1980, then to 24 months in 1988.[1]

Such long delays in obtaining judgment have become a cause of concern. Beyond a certain point, it can be said that 'justice delayed is justice denied'.[2] In a direct action, involving for example major

---

1 However, it should be said that the parties in direct actions are also often at the origin of some delay, as it has become common for them to ask for extensions of the time-limit to lodge their written pleadings.
2 See for example the comment of Professor H G Schermers in his article 'The European Court of First Instance', CML Rev 1988, p 541 at p 558: 'The backlog of the Court of Justice causes considerable damage to parties who cannot always afford delays and to the credibility of the law in general. A society that does not take the effective application of its legal system seriously is bound to undermine the law.'

1

TABLE I – FLOW OF PROCEEDINGS BEORE THE ECJ 1970–1988

	1970	1975	1980	1981	1982	1983	1984	1985	1986	1987	1988
Cases brought	79	130	279	323	345	297	312	433	329	395	373
Cases disposed of	*	*	206	210	329	275	340	331	324	380	386
(judgments delivered)	(64)	(78)	(132)	(128)	(185)	(151)	(165)	(211)	(174)	(208)	(238)
Cases pending at year end	*	*	328	441	465	489	465	574	592	618	605
Average duration of proceedings in months:											
preliminary rulings	*	6	9	12	12	12	14	14	15½	18	18
direct actions	*	9	18	12	13	14	17	20	21	22½	24

* Figures not available.

financial or commercial interests, it may cause parties substantial harm for the legal position to remain uncertain for two years or more. Preliminary rulings, although delivered by the ECJ somewhat more quickly than judgments in direct actions, are only a step in the proceedings before a national court, and the risk is that they might be felt to add disproportionately to the overall duration of proceedings. For the unity of the European Community legal order it would be particularly harmful if national courts and parties were deterred from seeking preliminary rulings by the prospect of a long delay in obtaining the ruling. Some commentators feel that 18 months is excessive and that something of the order of 12 months ought to be a maximum for the delivery of a preliminary ruling.[3]

Springing from that concern, various steps have been taken over the years to reduce the time taken to deal with the cases coming before the ECJ.[4] Those steps may be grouped under three heads: steps to increase the manpower of the ECJ, steps to streamline the procedure of the ECJ and steps to establish first instance tribunals.

Steps under all three heads were proposed by the ECJ to the Council in a memorandum of 21 July 1978.[5] As regards manpower, the ECJ asked the Council to increase the number of judges from nine to 12 and the number of Advocates General from four to six, pursuant to the fourth paragraph of Article 165 and the third paragraph of Article 166 of the Treaty.[6] The Council, however, merely granted one additional judge and one additional Advocate General.[7] Otherwise increases in the number of members[8] of the ECJ have corresponded to the successive enlargements of the European Communities from six to twelve Member States.[9] Thus the ECJ now has 13 judges: one for each

3 See eg 'Law Lord of Luxembourg', interview of Lord Mackenzie Stuart in the *Financial Times*, 3 October 1988.
4 On the historical background, see also 'Le Tribunal de Première Instance des Communautés Européennes' by R Joliet and W Vogel in *Revue du Marché Commun* 1989, p 423, and 'The Essential Minimum: The Establishment of the Court of First Instance' by T Kennedy in *European Law Review* 1989, p 7.
5 As to that memorandum, see the 17th Report of the House of Lords Select Committee on the European Communities, Session 1978–79, 'Staff Administrative Tribunal', paragraph 2; and 23rd Report of the House of Lords Select Committee on the European Communities, Session 1979–80, 'European Court of Justice', passim.
6 In this book, for the sake of simplicity, reference is made only to the provisions of the EEC Treaty ('the Treaty') as including the corresponding provisions of the ECSC and Euratom Treaties, and to the Protocol on the Statute of the Court of Justice of the EEC ('the Statute') as including the corresponding provisions of the ECSC and Euratom Statutes, unless the context requires otherwise.
7 Council Decisions Nos 81/208/Euratom, ECSC, EEC and 81/209/Euratom, ECSC, EEC, both of 30 March 1981 (OJ 1981 L 100, pp 20 and 21 respectively).
8 Ie the Judges and Advocates General.
9 The number of judges was increased from six to nine when Denmark, Ireland and the United Kingdom joined the Communities (1972 Act of Accession, Article 17; OJ

Member State with one more giving an odd number. And it has six Advocates General, which maintains the ratio at one Advocate General to two judges. At the same time the staff of the ECJ has grown steadily, numbering some 700 in 1988. In particular the staff now includes three legal secretaries (*'référendaires'*) for each member.[10] On the other hand, the ECJ has apparently never used the power to propose the appointment of Assistant Rapporteurs.[11]

Among procedural steps which have been taken, there may be mentioned in particular the more extensive use made of chambers. From the outset the EEC and Euratom Treaties have empowered the ECJ to form chambers of three or five judges to deal with certain categories of case.[12] Initially, however, the ECJ was not allowed to assign to a chamber any request for a preliminary ruling or any case brought by a Member State or a Community institution.[13] In 1974 that restriction was relaxed so as to allow certain preliminary rulings to be assigned to chambers.[14] By its memorandum of 1978 the ECJ asked the Council to agree to a further amendment of the rules so as to allow it to assign any type of case to chambers if it saw fit, but the Council was not prepared to go so far. The 1979 amendment to the ECJ's Rules of Procedure[15] widened the range of preliminary rulings which could be

---

(English Special Edition) 27 March 1972). When Greece joined the Communities, the number of judges was increased to 10 (Council Decision No 80/1313/EEC, Euratom, ECSC of 22 December 1980; OJ 1980 L 380, p 6). It was increased to 11 shortly afterwards by Council Decision No 81/208/Euratom, ECSC, EEC (mentioned in the preceding footnote). Finally, it was increased to 13 when Portugal and Spain joined the Communities (1985 Act of Accession, Article 17; OJ 1985 L 302, p 1).

The number of Advocates General was increased from two to four when Denmark, Ireland and the United Kingdom joined the Communities (1972 Act of Accession, Article 18; and Council Decision of 1 January 1973 increasing the number of Advocates General; OJ 1973 L 2, p 29). It was increased to five by Council Decision No 81/209/Euratom, ECSC, EEC (mentioned in the preceding footnote) and to six upon the accession of Portugal and Spain (1985 Act of Accession, Article 18).

10 Provision was made for a third legal secretary from 1986.
11 See Article 16 of the ECSC Statute, Articles 12 of the EEC and Euratom Statutes and Article 24 of the ECJ's Rules of Procedure.
12 EEC Treaty, Article 165, second paragraph; Euratom Treaty, Article 137, second paragraph. ECSC Treaty, Article 32, second paragraph, as amended by the Convention on Certain Institutions Common to the European Communities of 1957, is in identical terms.
13 ECSC Treaty, Article 32, third paragraph; EEC Treaty, Article 165, third paragraph; Euratom Treaty, Article 137, third paragraph.
14 Idem, as amended by Council Decision No 74/584/EEC, Euratom, ECSC of 26 November 1974 (OJ 1974 L 318, p 22); and ECJ Rules of Procedure, Article 95, as adopted in 1974 (OJ 1974 L 350, p 1).
15 OJ 1979 L 238, p 1. See in particular Article 95.

assigned to chambers[16] and allowed certain actions brought by natural or legal persons to be assigned to chambers in addition to staff cases. However, under the legislation as it currently stands, all cases brought by a Member State or a Community institution must still be heard by the full Court,[17] and the full Court must hear any case where a Member State or institution involved so requests.[18] In recent years the ECJ has increasingly tended to refer cases to chambers wherever possible; but further use of the chambers is limited by the present legislative restrictions.

A more recent initiative to streamline the ECJ's procedure which should also be mentioned is the imposition of stringent limits on the speaking time allowed to parties at hearings. The basic allocation is 15 minutes in three-judge chambers and 30 minutes in five-judge chambers or before the full Court, with an extension being possible on request supported by valid reasons.

In addition to changes in the ECJ's procedure and increases in its manpower, various proposals have been made to set up tribunals to take over part of the ECJ's jurisdiction at first instance. Suggestions for the establishment of a tribunal to take over the ECJ's jurisdiction at first instance in disputes between the Community institutions and their staff date back at least to the early 1970's. The Council agreed on its desirability in 1974 and again in 1978,[19] following which the Commission in 1978 submitted a proposal to the Council for the establishment of an administrative tribunal to deal with staff cases.[20] The jurisdiction arises under Article 179 of the Treaty and the Staff Regulations. The Commission's proposal was based on the view that the tribunal could be set up by amending the Staff Regulations, without necessitating the amendment of the Treaty. However, it was not adopted, owing to opposition from France and Ireland, who considered that the establishment of such a tribunal required the amendment of the Treaty.[1]

Separately from that proposal, the ECJ in its 1978 memorandum suggested to the Council that another tribunal might be set up to take over its jurisdiction at first instance in actions brought by private persons relating to competition matters and to the non-contractual

16 Under Article 95(1) all preliminary rulings may now be assigned to chambers in so far as the difficulty or the importance of the case or its particular circumstances do not require it to be dealt with by the full Court.
17 ECSC Treaty, Article 32, third paragraph; EEC Treaty, Article 165, third paragraph; Euratom Treaty, Article 137, third paragraph.
18 ECJ Rules of Procedure, Article 95(2), second sub-paragraph.
19 See 'Staff Administrative Tribunal' (cited at footnote 5 above), paragraph 3.
20 OJ 1978 C 225, p 6. On that proposal, see 'Staff Administrative Tribunal' (cited at footnote 5 above).
1 See Joliet and Vogel op cit, at p 425.

liability of the Community.[2] That suggestion was not taken up by the Council.

In March 1985 the President of the Commission, Mr Jacques Delors, in presenting to the European Parliament the Programme of the Commission for 1985, indicated that during 1985 it would propose the establishment of an administrative tribunal to hear at first instance actions against Commission decisions in competition matters and would submit another proposal for the establishment of an administrative tribunal to deal with staff cases.[3] However, events took a different turn.

An inter-governmental conference was held in Luxembourg in Autumn 1985 to prepare an agreement on the institutional reform of the Communities, which was ultimately adopted as the Single European Act. Reforms concerning the ECJ were not initially envisaged, but the ECJ suggested to the conference that provisions on the ECJ should be included in the amendments being prepared. When the conference agreed, the ECJ proposed the insertion in the Treaties of a provision empowering the Council to establish a court of first instance by a subsequent decision. The proposal was adopted rapidly and with little alteration. The Heads of Government of the European Communities reached agreement at their meeting in Luxembourg in December 1985. The Single European Act[4] was signed at Luxembourg on 17 February 1986 and at The Hague on 28 February 1986. After ratification, it came into force on 1 July 1987.

Measures for the establishment of the CFI

1. The New Article 168a of the Treaty

The Single European Act[5] inserted a new Article 168a and a new second paragraph into Article 188 of the EEC Treaty, and it inserted identically-worded provisions into the ECSC and Euratom Treaties.[6] Article 168a empowered the Council to establish a court of first instance and the new second paragraph of Article 188 empowered the Council to amend the provisions of Title III of the Statute of the ECJ, which is headed 'Procedure'.

2 On that suggestion, see 'European Court of Justice' (cited at footnote 5 above), in particular paragraphs 2, 36 to 39, and 50.
3 Programme of the Commission for 1985, paragraphs 32 and 133 (Bulletin of the European Communities, Supplement 4/85, pp 21 and 55).
4 OJ 1987 L 169, p 1.
5 Articles 4, 5, 11, 12, 26 and 27.
6 A new Article 32d and new second paragraph of Article 45 of the ECSC Treaty; a new Article 140a and a new second paragraph in Article 160 of the Euratom Treaty. See Appendix I for the text of these provisions.

Article 168a of the EEC Treaty largely predetermines the nature of the CFI. Article 168a(1) in particular provides: 'At the request of the Court of Justice and after consulting the Commission and the European Parliament, the Council may, acting unanimously, attach to the Court of Justice a court with jurisdiction to hear and determine at first instance, subject to a right of appeal to the Court of Justice on points of law only and in accordance with the conditions laid down by the Statute, certain classes of action or proceedings brought by natural or legal persons. That court shall not be competent to hear and determine actions brought by Member States or by Community institutions or questions referred for a preliminary ruling under Article 177.'

Three salient points emerge from that paragraph. First, the CFI is not to be a new institution or an autonomous body at all but is to be 'attached to the Court of Justice'.

Secondly, the jurisdiction of the CFI is defined as being 'to hear and determine at first instance . . . certain classes of action or proceeding brought by natural or legal persons'. It is not competent to deal with preliminary rulings or actions brought by Member States or Community institutions. The range of actions within the jurisdiction of the CFI is thus quite narrowly delimited from the outset, by reference to the type of procedure concerned. It is important to emphasise that these limitations on its jurisdiction will continue to apply indefinitely and can only be relaxed by an amendment to the Treaties.

Thirdly, the decision of the CFI at first instance is 'subject to a right of appeal to the Court of Justice on points of law only'. Thus it is provided that appeal may not be by way of a full re-hearing but is confined to 'points of law', although the exact meaning of that term is left to be defined subsequently.

For the rest, Article 168a lays down an outline of further measures applicable to the CFI. Article 168a(2) requires the Council to determine the composition of the CFI and make the necessary adjustments and additions to the Statute, but it stipulates that the provisions of the Treaty relating to the ECJ, in particular the provisions of the Statute, are to apply to the CFI unless the Council decides otherwise.[7] Article 168a(3) provides for the appointment of the members of the CFI. And Article 168a(4) provides that the CFI is to establish its own rules of procedure in agreement with the ECJ and subject to the unanimous approval of the Council.

---

7 That provision embodies a basic tendency towards maintaining similarity between the provisions on the two courts.

2. Other measures for the establishment of the CFI

Within that framework, four basic measures were needed to set up the CFI:

1. A decision of the Council establishing the CFI, determining its composition and adopting the necessary adjustments and additional provisions to the Statute. The ECJ submitted a proposal for such a decision to the Council on 29 September 1987.[8] The decision was adopted on 24 October 1988: Council Decision 88/591/ECSC, EEC, Euratom, establishing a Court of First Instance of the European Communities ('the Decision').[9]

The recitals to the Decision include a statement of the object of setting up the CFI, which is twofold. On the one hand, it is to improve the judicial protection of individual interests in cases requiring a close examination of complex facts.[10] On the other hand, it is to maintain the quality and effectiveness of judicial review in the Community legal order by allowing the ECJ to concentrate on the fundamental task of ensuring uniform interpretation of Community law.[11]

The Decision comprises 14 articles, which may be considered in three groups. First, Articles 1 to 4 provide for the establishment of the CFI, determine its composition, define its jurisdiction, and deal with the effects of its judgments and other essential judicial matters. A second group, Articles 5 to 10, inserts in the EEC Statute a new Title IV headed 'Court of First Instance of the European Communities' and consisting of Articles 44 to 54, and re-numbers the former Articles 44, 45 and 46 of that Statute Articles 55, 56 and 57 respectively. It makes substantially identical provision in relation to the ECSC and Euratom Statutes, except that the ECSC Statute is alone in containing sub-headings and the new articles of the Euratom Statute are numbered differently from those of the other two Statutes.[12] Thirdly, Articles 11 to 14 of the Decision deal with practical matters concerning the establishment of the CFI, such as the designation of the first President and the transfer of pending cases from the ECJ.

The Decision came into force on 26 November 1988, with the

---

8 On that proposal, see the 5th Report of the House of Lords Select Committee on the European Communities, Session 1987–88, 'A European Court of First Instance'.
9 OJ 1988 L 319, p 1; [1989] 1 CMLR 323. In view of discrepancies between, and terminological shortcomings in, certain language versions, a corrigendum to the Decision was issued (OJ 1989 L 241, p 4) and a corrected version published (OJ 1989 C 215, p 1; [1989] 3 CMLR 458). See Appendix II for the text of the Decision.
10 Fourth recital.
11 Fifth recital.
12 The ECSC Statute is dealt with by Articles 5 and 6 of the Decision, the EEC Statute by Articles 7 and 8, and the Euratom Statute by Articles 9 and 10.

exception of Article 3 which empowers the CFI to exercise its allotted jurisdiction.[13] That Article came into force on 31 October 1989.[14]

2. A Council regulation providing for the remuneration of the members of the CFI. The Council adopted a regulation to that effect on 19 December 1988.[15]

3. Amendments to the ECJ's Rules of Procedure to govern proceedings on appeals from the CFI. Such amendments are to be adopted by the ECJ subject to the unanimous approval of the Council.[16] Such amendments were unanimously approved by the Council on 29 May 1989 and were adopted by the ECJ on 7 June 1989.[17] They came into force on 18 August 1989.[18]

4. The CFI has to adopt its own Rules of Procedure in agreement with the ECJ and subject to the unanimous approval of the Council.[19] That process requires a certain amount of time. However, the third paragraph of Article 11 of the Decision provides that, 'until the entry into force of the Rules of Procedure of the Court of First Instance, the Rules of Procedure of the Court of Justice shall apply *mutatis mutandis*'.[20] Hence the CFI is allowed to start operations notwithstanding the absence of its own Rules of Procedure.[1]

Commencement of operation of the CFI

Article 13 of the Decision provides that Article 3 of the Decision is to

13 Decision, Article 13.
14 See below 'Commencement of Operation of the CFI'.
15 Council Regulation (ECSC, EEC, Euratom) No 4045/88 of 19 December 1988 laying down the emoluments of the President, Members and Registar of the Court of First Instance of the European Communities (OJ 1988 L 356, p 1).
16 Under what is now the third paragraph of Article 188 of the Treaty.
17 OJ 1989 L 241, p 1. See Appendix IV for the text of the amendments.
18 Amendments to the Rules of Procedure of the Court of Justice of the European Communities of 7 June 1989, Article 3.
19 Article 168a(4) of the Treaty. Moreover, the second paragraph of Article 11 of the Decision stipulates that the CFI shall adopt its Rules of Procedure 'immediately upon its constitution'.
20 See Appendix III for the text of the ECJ's Rules of Procedure prior to their amendment in 1989.
 1 The opposite applied to the Court of Justice of the ECSC when it was established. The third paragraph of Article 5 of the Convention on the Transitional Provisions, appended to the ECSC Treaty, provided: 'No matter may be brought before the Court until its rules of procedure have been published'. Similar provision was made in relation to the Court of Justice of the EEC by the third paragraph of Article 244 of the EEC Treaty and in relation to the Court of Justice of the EAEC by the third paragraph of Article 212 of the Euratom Treaty.

enter into force on the date of publication of a ruling by the President
of the ECJ that the CFI 'has been constituted in accordance with law'.
That ruling was published in the Official Journal of the European
Communities on 31 October 1989.[2] Thereupon, Article 3 of the
Decision, which defines the jurisdiction of the CFI, entered into force,
with the effect that from then on the cases within the defined
jurisdiction must be brought before the CFI.

Furthermore, under Article 14 of the Decision, cases within the
defined jurisdiction which were pending before the ECJ on the same
date and in which the Judge-Rapporteur's preliminary report had not
yet been presented were to be referred to the CFI. Pursuant to that
provision 151 cases fell to be transferred to the CFI as at 31 October
1989.[3] Thus the CFI commenced operating immediately with a
substantial caseload of its own and did not have to wait for cases
gradually to be lodged before it.

2 OJ 1989 L 317, p 48.
3 See Table IV below.

2 The composition and organisation of the CFI

The members

The CFI consists of twelve 'members'.[1] The ECJ proposed seven, but it was unlikely that the Council in determining the composition of the CFI under Article 168a(2) would settle for fewer than twelve members, corresponding to the number of Member States. That is a relatively large membership, considering that the ECJ itself consists of only nineteen members.

Article 168a(3) of the Treaty provides that the members of the CFI shall be chosen from persons whose independence is beyond doubt and who possess 'the ability required for appointment to judicial office'. That requirement may be compared to the slightly different criterion in Article 167 of the Treaty, according to which members of the ECJ shall be chosen from persons whose independence is beyond doubt and who possess 'the qualifications required for appointment to the highest judicial offices in their respective countries or who are jurisconsults of recognised competence'. That difference in wording may be taken to reflect a concern that the members of the CFI should, on the one hand, be of sufficient calibre to ensure the authority of the new court and, on the other hand, have the practical ability to carry out the tasks of a first instance jurisdiction, in particular fact-finding. Certainly such an intention was evinced in the proposal and in the course of the discussions which led up to the adoption of the Decision establishing the CFI.

Article 168a(3) also provides that the members of the CFI are appointed by common accord of the Governments of the Member States for a term of six years, that the membership is partially renewed every three years and that retiring members are eligible for reappointment.[2] Pursuant to that provision, the first members of the CFI were appointed as from 1 September 1989 by a Decision of the

1 Decision, Article 2(1). Cf EEC Treaty, Articles 165 and 166, whereby the ECJ consists of thirteen judges assisted by six Advocates General.
2 Similar provisions apply to the members of the ECJ: cf Article 167 of the Treaty.

representatives of the Governments of the Member States of the European Communities of 18 July 1989.[3] Although they are not bound by any nationality requirement, the Member States appointed one member from each Member State.

The first members of the CFI are the following:

The Hon. Mr Justice Donal Barrington (Ireland)
born on 28 February 1928, Judge of the Irish High Court since 1979 and Member of the Special Criminal Court since 1987, previously Senior Counsel specialising in constitutional and commercial law.

Mr Jacques Biancarelli (France)
born on 18 October 1948, Director of Legal Services at Crédit Lyonnais, former legal secretary at the ECJ.

Mr Cornelis Briët (Netherlands)
born on 23 February 1944, Vice-President of the District Court of Rotterdam, Deputy Judge at the District Court of Middelburg and Deputy Judge at the Cantonal courts of Rotterdam, Brielle and Sommelsdijk.

Professor David Edward, CMG, QC (United Kingdom)
born on 14 November 1934, Salvesen Professor of European Institutions at the University of Edinburgh, Honorary Sheriff at Perth and Chairman of Medical Appeal Tribunals.

Mr Rafael García-Valdecasas y Fernandez (Spain)
born in 1946, Spanish Government lawyer responsible for litigation before the ECJ and for negotiations on the establishment of the CFI.

Mr Heinrich Kirschner (Federal Republic of Germany)
born on 7 January 1938, senior official in the Federal Ministry of Justice, earlier a judge in the Regional Court of Bochum and the Local Court of Wanne-Eickel.

Mr Koenraad Lenaerts (Belgium)
born in 1954, Professor of Law at the Katholieke Universiteit Leuven, Visiting Professor at the University of Strasbourg and Professor at the College of Europe Bruges, former legal secretary at the ECJ.

Mr Antonio Saggio (Italy)
born in 1934, Judge of the Court of Cassation and Professor of Community Law at the Scuola Superiore della Pubblica Amministrazione in Rome, former legal secretary at the ECJ.

Mr Romain Schintgen (Luxembourg)
born on 22 March 1939, senior official in the Luxembourg Ministry of Labour, expert in labour law.

3 Decision 89/452/EEC, Euratom, ECSC (OJ 1989 L 220, p 76).

Mr Bo Vesterdorf (Denmark)
born in 1945, senior official in the Danish Ministry of Justice, former lawyer-linguist at the ECJ.

Mr José Luis da Cruz Vilaça (Portugal)
born on 20 September 1944, Professor of European Economy and International Economic Organisations at Lusiada University, former Advocate General at the ECJ.

Mr Christos Yeraris (Greece)
born on 13 September 1938, Member of the Greek Council of State and lecturer in Community law at the National School of Public Administration and the Institute of Continuing Education.

In order to ensure the partial renewal of the membership of the CFI every three years in accordance with Article 168a(3) of the Treaty, half of those members were appointed for six years and the other half for three years.[4] Those whose terms of office were to expire at the end of the first three years[5] were chosen by lot by the President of the Council.[6] They may, however, be reappointed.[7] A member of the CFI may also resign before his term of office has expired, in which case his successor is appointed for the remainder of his term not for a fresh term of three or six years.[8]

Before taking up his duties each member of the CFI must take an oath before the ECJ to perform his duties impartially and conscientiously and to preserve the secrecy of the deliberations of the CFI.[9] He must also give a solemn undertaking that, both during and after his term of office, he will respect the obligations arising therefrom, in particular the duty to behave with integrity and discretion as regards the acceptance of certain appointments or benefits after he has ceased to hold office. The members of the CFI may not hold any political or administrative office, nor may they engage in any occupation unless exemption is exceptionally granted by the Council. Any doubt as to these matters falls to be settled by a decision of the ECJ adopted after hearing the CFI.[10] The first members of the CFI took the oath and signed the solemn declaration before the ECJ on 25 September 1989.

4 Decision 89/452/EEC, Euratom, ECSC, Article 1, second paragraph.
5 Messrs Briët, Lenaerts, Schintgen, Vesterdorf, da Cruz Vilaça and Yeraris: Decision of the President of the Council of 3 October 1989 (OJ 1989 C273, p. 3).
6 Pursuant to the Decision establishing the CFI, Article 12, and to Decision 89/452/ EEC, Euratom, ECSC, Article 1, third paragraph.
7 Treaty, Article 168a(3).
8 Statute, Articles 5 and 7, applied to the CFI by Statute, Article 44.
9 Statute, Articles 2 and 44; see also ECJ Rules of Procedure, Article 3(1).
10 Statute, Articles 4 and 44; see also ECJ Rules of Procedure, Article 3(2).

No member of the CFI may take part in the disposal of any case in which he has previously been involved in another capacity. If a member of the CFI takes the view that he should not take part in a case, he so informs the President of the CFI. If the President considers that a member of the CFI should not take part in a case, he notifies the member accordingly. Any difficulty as to the application of those rules is settled by a decision of the CFI.[11] A member of the CFI may be deprived of his office or of his right to a pension if, in the unanimous opinion of the judges and Advocates General of the ECJ adopted after hearing the CFI, he no longer fulfils the requisite conditions or meets the obligations arising from his office.[12]

The members of the CFI are immune from legal proceedings, and after they have ceased to hold office they continue to enjoy immunity in respect of acts performed by them in their official capacity, including words spoken or written. The immunity may be waived by the ECJ, sitting in plenary session, after hearing the CFI.[13]

They also enjoy the privileges and immunities granted to officials of the European Communities.[14] Apart from immunity in respect of acts performed in an official capacity, these include exemption from immigration restrictions and formalities for the registration of aliens in each Member State and the right to import their furniture and effects duty-free on taking up their duties in the country concerned.[15] The members of the CFI are required to reside at the place where the CFI has its seat, ie Luxembourg.[16] The remuneration of the members of the CFI is determined by the Council.[17] Like the remuneration of Community officials, it is exempt from national taxes but subject to a tax for the benefit of the Communities.[18]

---

11 Statute, Article 16, first, second and third paragraphs, applied to the CFI by Statute, Article 44.
12 Statute, Articles 6 and 44; see also ECJ Rules of Procedure, Article 4.
13 Statute, Articles 3 and 44.
14 Decision, Article 2(5), applying to the members of the CFI Article 21 of the Protocol on the Privileges and Immunities of the European Communities. Article 21 in turn refers to Articles 12 to 15 and 18 of the same Protocol.
15 Protocol on Privileges and Immunities, Article 12, applied by idem Article 21 and Decision, Article 2(5).
16 Statute, Article 13, applied to the members of the CFI by Statute, Article 44.
17 Treaty establishing a Single Council and a Single Commission of the European Communities, Article 6, applied to the members of the CFI by Decision, Article 2(5). The emoluments of the members of the CFI were laid down, pursuant to those provisions, by Council Regulation (ECSC, EEC, Euratom) No 4045/88 of 19 December 1988 (OJ 1988 L 356, p 1).
18 Protocol on Privileges and Immunities, Article 13, applied by idem Article 21 and Decision, Article 2(5). The tax for the benefit of the Communities is provided for in Council Regulation (EEC, Euratom, ECSC) No 260/68 of 29 February 1968 (OJ English Special Edition 1968 (I), p 37), as amended.

The President

The Portuguese member of the CFI, Mr da Cruz Vilaça, was appointed President of the CFI for three years as from 1 September 1989. He was appointed by common accord of the Governments of the Member States pursuant to the first paragraph of Article 11 of the Decision.[19] That mode of appointment applies only to the first President of the CFI. Subsequent Presidents fall to be elected by the members of the CFI from among their number for a term of three years. They may be re-elected.[20]

Advocates General

In the process of determining the composition of the CFI, much discussion was aroused by the question of whether the CFI should be given Advocates General. In its proposal the ECJ did not make provision for Advocates General in the CFI but only judges, taking the view that the fundamental role of the Advocates General at the ECJ, that of assisting the ECJ in the development of Community law, was not indispensable in the CFI. On the other hand, the European Parliament[1] considered that the CFI should be assisted by three Advocates General in addition to having twelve judges. The Commission[2] likewise declared itself in favour of the inclusion of Advocates General in the CFI. The trade unions of Community staff as well as voices within the legal professions in the Member States also favoured the provision of Advocates General in the CFI.

Opinions within the Council itself were divided. Agreement could not be reached either on the total absence of Advocates General from the CFI or on their appointment for a fixed term in addition to judges. In the end, the Council adopted a compromise between the two positions: Article 2(3) of the Decision provides that the members of the CFI 'may be called upon to perform the task of an Advocate General'. Although it is not excluded that members of the CFI might

19 Decision of the representatives of the Governments of the Member States of the European Communities of 18 July 1989 No 89/452/EEC, Euratom, ECSC (OJ 1989 L 220, p 76).
20 Decision, Article 2(2).
 1 Opinion of the European Parliament on the ECJ Proposal (OJ 1988 C 187, p 223).
 2 'Preliminary Guidelines adopted by the Commission for the Preparation of an Opinion on the Proposal by the Court of Justice for a Council decision establishing a Court of First Instance and Amending the Statutes of the Court of Justice' (Commission document SEC (1988) 366 final, 18 May 1988, p 6 bis), confirmed in the Commission's formal opinion of 20 July 1988 (Commission document SEC (1988) 1121 final).

be appointed Advocates General for a period of time, it seems to be envisaged rather that they should be chosen on a case-by-case basis.[3] Neither the way in which the cases should be selected nor the way in which the members of the CFI should be chosen for the task of an Advocate General is specified in the Decision. The third sub-paragraph of Article 2(3) of the Decision provides that the criteria for selecting cases in which an Advocate General is to deliver an Opinion, as well as the procedures for designating the Advocates General, shall be laid down in the Rules of Procedure of the CFI. The Council Decision has thus provided for the presence of Advocates General before the CFI but left the CFI to resolve the outstanding practical difficulties itself.

The duties of the Advocate General before the CFI are described in identical terms to those of the Advocate General before the ECJ.[4] The Advocate General, acting with complete impartiality and independence, is to make, in open court, reasoned submissions on certain cases brought before the CFI in order to assist the CFI in the performance of its task. Just as an Advocate General before the ECJ does not take part in the deliberations of that court, a member called upon to perform the task of Advocate General in a case before the CFI may not take part in the judgment of the case.[5]

Sittings of the CFI, Plenary Sessions and Chambers

The CFI remains permanently in session. The duration of the judicial vacations is to be determined by the CFI with due regard to the needs of its business.[6]

Article 2(4) of the Decision provides that the CFI *shall* sit in Chambers of three or five judges, and that it *may* sit in plenary session in certain cases.[7] The ECJ's proposal did not allow for the CFI to sit in plenary session, neither did the Commission or the European Parliament think it necessary. However, the view was taken in the Council that it should be open to the CFI to sit in plenary session in

---

3 Cf the words 'reasoned submissions on certain cases' in the second sub-paragraph of Article 2(3) of the Decision.
4 Decision, Article 2(3), second sub-paragraph; cf Treaty, Article 166, second paragraph.
5 Decision, Article 2(3), fourth sub-paragraph; cf ECJ Rules of Procedure, Article 27(2).
6 Statute, Article 14, applied to the CFI by Statute, Article 44.
7 Thus the basic rule for the CFI is the converse of that for the ECJ. The CFI is to sit in Chambers save in cases for which specific provision is made, whereas the ECJ is to sit in plenary session save in particular categories of cases for which rules are laid down; cf ECSC Treaty, Article 32, second paragraph, EEC Treaty, Article 165, second paragraph, and Euratom Treaty, Article 137, second paragraph.

particularly important cases. The composition of the Chambers, the assignment of cases to the Chambers and the definition of the cases in which the CFI may sit in plenary session are all left open by the Decision, which provides that those matters are to be governed by the Rules of Procedure of the CFI.[8] The ECJ's Rules of Procedure, which apply *mutatis mutandis* until the CFI adopts its own Rules of Procedure, provide a procedure for the assignment of cases to Chambers,[9] but the essential criteria remain to be established by the CFI in due time. In dealing with these matters, the CFI may also consider whether to make formal provision for specialisation of its Chambers by subject-matter, in particular specialisation in staff cases on the one hand and 'economic law' cases on the other.

The quorum both for a plenary session and for a Chamber is, however, already established. Decisions of the CFI are valid only when an uneven number of its members is sitting in the deliberations (notwithstanding that the total membership of the CFI is an even number). Decisions of the full court are valid if seven members are sitting. Decisions of the Chambers are valid only if three judges are sitting.[10] If one of the judges of a Chamber is prevented from attending, a judge of another Chamber may be called upon to sit in accordance with conditions laid down in the Rules of Procedure.[11] However, a party may not apply for a change in the composition of the CFI in plenary session or of one of its Chambers on the grounds either of the nationality of one of the judges sitting on a case or of the absence from the plenary session or Chamber of a judge of the nationality of that party.[12]

The Registrar

The CFI appoints its Registrar and lays down the rules governing his service.[13] The Registrar of the CFI takes an oath before the CFI to perform his duties impartially and conscientiously and to preserve the secrecy of the deliberations of the CFI.[14] The CFI arranges for its

8 For its first year of operation the CFI decided on 4 October 1989 to set up two Chambers of five judges and three Chambers of three judges and in principle to assign staff cases to the latter and other cases to the former (OJ 1989 C 281, p 12).
9 See below in Chapter 4 'Procedure before the CFI'.
10 Statute, Article 15, applied to the CFI by Statute, Article 44.
11 Statute, Article 15, applied to the CFI by Statute, Article 44.
12 Statute, Article 16, fourth paragraph, applied to the CFI by Statute, Article 44.
13 Statute, Article 45, first paragraph. The CFI appointed Mr Hans Jung as its Registrar by a decision of 26 September 1989 (OJ 1989 C 281, p 12).
14 Statute, Article 9, applied to the Registrar of the CFI *mutatis mutandis* by Statute, Article 45, first paragraph. Mr Jung took the oath as Registrar on 10 October 1989.

Registrar to be replaced on occasions when he is prevented from attending the CFI.[15] The Registrar of the CFI is required, as are its members, to reside at the place where the CFI has its seat, ie Luxembourg.[16] Like the members of the CFI, the Registrar of the CFI enjoys the privileges and immunities granted to officials of the European Communities and his remuneration is determined by the Council.[17]

The Registrar of the CFI is in charge of the Registry of the CFI, which is a separate one from that of the ECJ. That arrangement is based on the assumption that, in order to ensure its judicial independence, the CFI needs a separate Registry from that of the ECJ.

Administrative organisation

The CFI is 'attached to' the ECJ, and its seat is at the ECJ.[18] In a physical sense the attachment of the CFI to the ECJ is tangible, as both courts occupy the same group of buildings in Luxembourg. The CFI is at present housed in Annex A to the main building of the ECJ.[19] A second annex (Annex B) is under construction and a third annex (Annex C) is planned. Even though there may be some redistribution between these buildings in time, the two courts are likely to remain housed in the same complex of buildings, as they are at present.

The CFI does not have an administrative 'infrastructure' of its own but uses the departments of the ECJ. They comprise the translation, interpretation, library, research and documentation, legal data processing, personnel, finance and internal services departments. The only staff specifically working for the CFI are the staff of its own Registry and the personal staff of its members (at present one secretary and one legal secretary each).

Even the staff working specifically for the CFI are not appointed by the CFI itself but, as officials or other servants attached to the ECJ, render their services to the CFI under conditions agreed between the

---

15 Statute, Article 10, applied to the Registrar of the CFI *mutatis mutandis* by Statute, Article 45, first paragraph.
16 Statute, Article 13, applied to the Registrar of the CFI *mutatis mutandis* by Statute, Article 45, first paragraph.
17 Article 21 of the Protocol on Privileges and Immunities and Article 6 of the Treaty establishing a Single Council and a Single Commission of the European Communities, applied to the members and Registrar of the CFI by Decision, Article 2(5). The emoluments of the Registrar of the CFI were laid down by Council Regulation (ECSC, EEC, Euratom) No 4045/88 of 19 December 1988 (OJ 1988 L 356, p 1).
18 Decision, Article 1.
19 Called the 'Palais' in French.

President of the ECJ and the President of the CFI.[20] In order to ensure the independence of the CFI, it is provided that certain officials or other servants such as these, who would otherwise come under the direct authority of the ECJ, are responsible to the Registrar of the CFI under the authority of the President of the CFI.[1]

---

20 Statute, Article 45, second paragraph.
 1 Statute, Article 45, second paragraph; cf Statute, Article 11.

3 The jurisdiction of the CFI

Introduction

The jurisdiction of the CFI is defined in Article 3 and in certain respects also in Article 4 of the Decision. It is clear from the terms of Article 3 that the jurisdiction of the CFI excludes that of the ECJ. Article 3 provides: 'The Court of First Instance shall exercise at first instance the jurisdiction conferred on the Court of Justice' in certain defined categories of action. Within those categories, cases must be brought at first instance before the CFI and may not be brought before the ECJ.[1] That rule ensures respect for the principle of the 'lawful judge' which is important in the legal thinking of certain continental Member States, in particular the Federal Republic of Germany.[2] According to that principle it is of fundamental importance that the citizen should be able to know in advance who will be his judge, the matter being laid down by law and not left to the discretion of the authorities. Thus Article 3 eschews any arrangement whereby, for instance, cases might be brought before the ECJ and be referred to the CFI at the discretion of the ECJ.[3] The jurisdiction of the CFI is thus a compulsory jurisdiction.

Within the range determined by Article 168a(1) of the Treaty,[4] Article 3 of the Decision specifies four categories of case in which the CFI is to exercise at first instance the jurisdiction conferred on the ECJ by the Treaties and the legislation adopted in implementation of the Treaties. Those categories are:

1 As to the procedures giving effect to that rule, see Article 47 of the Statute and comments thereon in Chapter 4 'Procedure before the CFI'.
2 Where the principle is known as that of the 'gesetzlicher Richter'.
3 The only provision allowing for a case to be transferred from one court to the other is the provision contained in the third paragraph of Article 47 of the Statute to the effect that: 'Where applications are made [before the ECJ and before the CFI] for the same act to be declared void, the Court of First Instance may also decline jurisdiction in order that the Court of Justice may rule on such applications'. In those particular circumstances it seems that economy of procedure and the avoidance of conflicting decisions by the two courts are the predominant considerations.
4 Ie 'certain classes of action or proceeding brought by natural or legal persons'.

1) Staff cases;
2) Actions by undertakings against the Commission concerning individual acts relating to the application of the ECSC Treaty provisions on levies, production controls, price regulation or competition;
3) Actions by natural or legal persons against a Community institution relating to the implementation of the EEC competition rules applicable to undertakings;
4) Damages claims by natural or legal persons where the damage is alleged to arise from an act or failure to act which is the subject of an action under 1, 2 or 3 above.

In addition, Article 4 of the Decision provides for the CFI to have unlimited jurisdiction in regard to penalties, gives it jurisdiction to entertain a plea of illegality and empowers it to suspend measures and grant other interim relief. These heads of jurisdiction will now be considered in more detail.

Staff cases

Staff cases have been long an obvious category to remove from the jurisdiction of the ECJ at first instance. They differ clearly from the other types of litigation dealt with by the ECJ, in that they have a separate legal basis in Article 179 of the EEC Treaty[5] and are not directly concerned with the law on European integration. Since the disputes usually concern the terms of employment of individuals and not infrequently involve disputes on matters of fact, the litigation is of a kind more appropriate for a labour court than for a court such as the ECJ. As Table II shows, staff cases are also relatively numerous,[6] and they have taken up a substantial amount of the ECJ's time. Accordingly, after a number of earlier proposals had come to nothing,[7] jurisdiction to hear staff cases at first instance was transferred to the CFI by Article 3(1)(a) of the Decision.

Article 3(1)(a) gives the CFI jurisdiction at first instance over disputes between the Communities and their servants referred to in Article 179 of the EEC Treaty and in Article 152 of the Euratom Treaty.[8] Those

---

5 Along with Articles 90 and 91 of the Staff Regulations.
6 In absolute terms the average number of staff cases brought has increased in the 1980s as compared with the 1970s, although as a proportion of the ECJ's case load, staff cases have dropped from around one-third in the 1970s to less than one-fifth in the late 1980s.
7 See under 'Historical Background' in Chapter 1.
8 The ECSC Treaty contains no express provision in this regard.

TABLE II – STAFF CASES IN RELATION TO THE TOTAL NUMBER OF CASES
BROUGHT BEFORE THE ECJ 1970–1988

	Total Number of Cases brought before the ECJ	Staff Cases brought before the ECJ	Percentage of Total represented by Staff Cases
1970	79	35	44
1971	96	46	48
1972	82	23	28
1973	192	100	52
1974	102	41	40
1975	130	26	20
1976	126	19	15
1977	158	24	15
1978	268	22	8
1979	202*	43*	21
1980	279	116	42
1981	323	94	29
1982	345	85	25
1983	297	68	23
1984	312	43	14
1985	433	65	15
1986	329	57	17
1987	395	77	19
1988	373	58	16

* Adjusted to allow for several hundred related staff cases brought in 1979. Unadjusted figures for 1979: total number of cases brought 1,322; staff cases brought 1,163.

provisions, in identical terms, provide for jurisdiction 'in any dispute between the Community and its servants within the limits and under the conditions laid down in the Staff Regulations or the Conditions of Employment'. Those limits and conditions are laid down in Articles 90 and 91 of the Staff Regulations of Officials,[9] which are applied by analogy to other categories of employees by the Conditions of Employment of Other Servants.[10]

The Staff Regulations and the Conditions of Employment apply to

9 The Staff Regulations of Officials and the Conditions of Employment of Other Servants of the European Communities are laid down by Council Regulation (EEC, Euratom, ECSC) No 259/68 of 29 February 1968 (OJ English Special Edition 1968 (I), p 30), as amended.
10 Conditions of Employment of Other Servants, Articles 46, 73 and 83.

the four institutions of the Communities[11] and to the Economic and Social Committee and the Court of Auditors.[12] In addition, certain bodies which are separate from the institutions include in their conditions of employment disputes provisions which follow the same pattern.[13] Furthermore, the ECJ has held that its jurisdiction in staff disputes is not restricted to the institutions as just defined but also includes the European Investment Bank as a Community institution established and with a legal personality conferred by the EEC Treaty.[14] Thus it is thought that the jurisdiction conferred on the CFI by Article 3(1)(a) of the Decision falls to be interpreted as covering the widest range of Community organizations as employers, notwithstanding that the terms of Article 179 of the EEC Treaty, Article 152 of the Euratom Treaty and the Staff Regulations, read literally, may appear somewhat narrower.

Under the Staff Regulations the ECJ (and hence the CFI) has jurisdiction in disputes between the Communities and any person to whom the Regulations apply.[15] That category includes not only present officials of the Communities but also former officials, persons claiming the status of officials and unsuccessful candidates for recruitment as officials.[16] In addition, cases may be brought by persons having a claim in their own right under the Staff Regulations, such as divorced spouses, widows, widowers and orphans of deceased officials.[17] As a general rule, such persons may bring an action only if they have first submitted a complaint to the appointing authority of their institution and that complaint has been rejected.[18] The action must be brought within three months of the rejection of the complaint.[19]

The CFI has jurisdiction to review the legality of an act adversely affecting the person concerned, and in disputes of a financial character

11 The Commission, the Council, the ECJ and the European Parliament.
12 Staff Regulations, Article 1.
13 Eg the European Centre for the Development of Vocational Training (Council Regulation No 1859/76, Arts 43 and 44; OJ 1976 L 214, p 1) and the European Foundation for the Improvement of Living and Working Conditions (Council Regulation No 1860/76, Arts 43 and 44; OJ 1976 L 214, p 24).
14 Case 110/75 *Mills v European Investment Bank* [1976] ECR 955 (admissibility), [1976] ECR 1613 (merits).
15 Staff Regulations, Article 91(1).
16 See eg Joined Cases 81–88/74 *Marenco v Commission* [1975] ECR 1247, ECJ; Case 116/78 *Bellintani v Commission* [1979] ECR 1585, ECJ; and Case 130/75 *Prais v Council* [1976] ECR 1589, ECJ.
17 See eg Case 24/71 *Meinhardt, (née Forderung) v Commission* [1972] ECR 269; Case 40/79 *Mrs P v Commission* [1981] ECR 361; and Joined Cases 75, 117/82 *Razzouk and Beydoun v Commission* [1984] ECR 1509.
18 Staff Regulations, Article 91(2). An exception is provided for in Article 91(4) whereby an action may be brought immediately after the complaint has been submitted if it is accompanied by an application for the suspension of the contested measure or other interim relief.
19 Staff Regulations, Article 91(3).

it has unlimited jurisdiction.[20] Under the latter kind of jurisdiction the CFI may award damages[1] and is free to substitute its own view for that of the defendant administration. The transfer of jurisdiction in staff cases effected by Article 3(1)(a) of the Decision thus includes actions for damages in so far as they are brought under Articles 90 and 91 of the Staff Regulations.

Coal and steel cases

Article 3(1)(b) of the Decision transfers to the CFI the ECJ's jurisdiction to hear at first instance annulment actions and actions for failure to act brought under the ECSC Treaty by undertakings or associations of undertakings concerning individual acts of the Commission relating to the application of the ECSC Treaty rules on levies, production controls, price regulation and competition.

The applicants in such actions do not comprise undertakings at large but only undertakings which produce coal or steel,[2] as well as associations of such undertakings referred to in Article 48 of the ECSC Treaty. The only possible defendant is the Commission.[3] Article 33 of the ECSC Treaty allows undertakings or associations of undertakings to bring an action for the annulment of decisions or recommendations concerning them which are individual in character. It also allows them to bring such an action against general decisions or recommendations which they consider to involve a misuse of powers affecting them,[4] but it seems that that part of the jurisdiction has not been transferred to the CFI.[5]

An annulment action under the ECSC Treaty lies on the same grounds as one under the EEC Treaty. However, it must be brought within one month, as compared with two months under the EEC Treaty.[6] The action for failure to act under the ECSC Treaty also

---

20 Staff Regulations, Article 91(1).
 1 Before the ECJ, see eg Case 48/76 *Reinarz v Commission and Council* [1977] ECR 291 at 298.
 2 ECSC Treaty, Article 80. That Article also provides that, in relation to Articles 65 and 66 of the ECSC Treaty (competition), undertakings include those engaged in distribution other than retail distribution.
 3 ECSC Treaty, Articles 33 and 35, reflected in the wording of Decision, Article 3(1)(b). Cf EEC Treaty, Articles 173 and 175, under which the Council may also be a defendant, reflected in the wording of Decision, Article 3(1)(c).
 4 ECSC Treaty, Article 33, second paragraph.
 5 Article 3(1)(b) of the Decision refers only to 'actions brought . . . by undertakings or by associations of undertakings . . . which concern individual acts . . .'
 6 ECSC Treaty, Article 33, third paragraph. Cf EEC Treaty, Article 173, third paragraph.

differs in a number of respects from its counterpart under the EEC Treaty. One important difference is that, when the institution concerned has been called upon to act, it cannot extract itself merely by 'defining its position' but must adopt a decision or recommendation, itself subject to an action for annulment,[7] which represents a more thorough provision for judicial review.

Before the CFI, actions of either kind may be brought concerning individual acts relating to the application of Article 50 and Articles 57 to 66 of the ECSC Treaty.[8] Article 50 concerns the imposition of levies on producers to finance the activities of the Commission. Articles 57 to 59 concern the control of production. Article 58 in particular allows the Commission in a period of manifest crisis to intervene directly and establish a system of quotas. Under that provision the Commission introduced a system of production quotas in 1980 in order to deal with recession and over-capacity in the steel sector. The Commission extended the system by a series of decisions until the end of 1988, by which time the crisis was largely past. Articles 60 to 64 concern the regulation of prices; and Articles 65 and 66 concern competition, in the sense of agreements and concentrations. The rules in all these areas comprise a power for the Commission to impose fines or other pecuniary penalties.[9] In that connection, the Decision also gives the CFI unlimited jurisdiction in appeals against pecuniary sanctions and periodic penalty payments.[10] Like an action for annulment, an appeal against a pecuniary sanction must be brought within one month.[11]

Over recent years the ECJ has had to deal with a large number of cases stemming from the system of production quotas introduced in 1980. Such cases frequently involve complex, technical legislation and detailed questions of fact. The number of cases is now diminishing, and may be expected to continue to do so following the expiry of the quota system. Thus the immediate prospect is that cases in this category will not be very numerous before the CFI, although as with any other category of litigation it is impossible to foretell whether it might flare up again in the future.

EEC competition cases

The third category of case transferred to CFI by the Decision is competition cases under the EEC Treaty. Article 3(1)(c) of the

7 ECSC Treaty, Article 35, third paragraph. Cf EEC Treaty, Article 175, second paragraph.
8 Decision, Article 3(1)(b).
9 See ECSC Treaty, Articles 50(3), 58(4), 64, 65(5) and 66(6).
10 Decision, Article 4, applying ECSC Treaty, Article 36, to the CFI.
11 ECSC Statute, Article 39, first paragraph, applied to the CFI by idem, Article 46.

Decision transfers to the CFI the ECJ's jurisdiction at first instance over actions for annulment and actions for failure to act brought by natural or legal persons under the EEC Treaty relating to the implementation of the competition rules applicable to undertakings. In the EEC Treaty the competition rules applicable to undertakings are Articles 85 to 90, which comprise provisions on agreements between undertakings and abuse of a dominant position by an undertaking as well as specific provisions for public undertakings and undertakings having monopoly rights.[12] The competition rules applicable to undertakings do not, however, include the rules on State aids, which are contained in Articles 92 to 94 of the Treaty.[13]

Under Article 173 of the EEC Treaty a natural or legal person may bring an annulment action against the Council or the Commission in respect of a decision addressed to him without having to establish any further interest in the action, but such a person may challenge a decision addressed to another person or a regulation only if he can prove that it is of direct and individual concern to him, which is a stringent condition to fulfil.[14] The action lies on grounds of lack of competence, infringement of an essential procedural requirement, infringement of the Treaty or of any rule of law relating to its application, or misuse of powers.[15] It must be brought within two months.[16]

Article 175 of the Treaty makes provision for actions for a declaration that the Council or the Commission has, in infringement of the Treaty, failed to act.[17] The action may be brought only if the institution has first been called upon to act and has failed to 'define its position' within two months of being so called upon.[18] A natural or legal person may bring such an action only if his complaint is that the institution has failed to address to him an act other than a recommendation or an opinion.[19] For the action to succeed, it appears that the institution must be under an obligation to adopt the act in question and not merely have a power to do so.[20] The circumstances in which those conditions may be fulfilled in the context of the competition rules applicable to undertakings are narrow.

Accordingly, the cases coming before the CFI under the present head of jurisdiction will generally consist of actions by undertakings

12 Articles 85, 86 and 90, respectively.
13 See further 'Matters Excluded from the Jurisdiction of the CFI', below.
14 EEC Treaty, Article 173, second paragraph.
15 EEC Treaty, Article 173, first paragraph.
16 EEC Treaty, Article 173, third paragraph.
17 EEC Treaty, Article 175, first paragraph.
18 EEC Treaty, Article 175, second paragraph.
19 EEC Treaty, Article 175, third paragraph.
20 See, before the ECJ, Case 125/78 *GEMA v Commission* [1979] ECR 3173, ECJ, and Case 246/81 *Bethell v Commission* [1982] ECR 2277, ECJ.

contesting Commission decisions affecting them. Thus a case such as *British Leyland*[1] contesting a fine imposed by a Commission decision is now within the jurisdiction of the CFI. A number of major decisions in the field of competition have been taken in cases of this type.[2] Although the power of decision in such major cases at first instance now lies with the CFI, the ECJ retains jurisdiction over the same questions where the case arises by way of a reference for a preliminary ruling. Thus, for example, a case such as Case T-66/89 *Publishers' Association v Commission* contesting the Commission's decision against the British Net Book Agreements now falls to be heard by the CFI, whereas a case such as *Binon*[3] concerning the arrangements for the distribution of newspapers and periodicals in Belgium, and thus raising similar and equally sensitive issues, will remain before the ECJ. While in principle the ECJ retains ultimate control over the evolution of the case-law on competition by virtue of its power to decide on appeals, that remains dependent on an appeal being lodged in a particular case.

Claims for the annulment of Commission decisions imposing fines on undertakings for breach of the EEC competition rules have regularly been coupled, in the alternative, with a claim for a reduction in the amount of the fine pursuant to Article 172 of the EEC Treaty[4] and Regulation 17.[5] Article 4 of the Decision provides *inter alia* that Article 172 of the EEC Treaty 'shall apply to the Court of First Instance', the effect of which in conjunction with Regulation 17 is to grant the CFI unlimited jurisdiction to cancel, reduce or increase the amount of a competition fine as well as jurisdiction to annul a decision imposing such a fine.

Related damages claims

Actions for the annulment of a measure are not infrequently linked to a claim for compensation in respect of damage allegedly caused by the same measure. Since the two claims arise out of essentially the same facts, it is astute for the same court to deal with both claims. That is the purpose of the fourth head of jurisdiction defined by the Decision.

---

1 Case 226/84 *British Leyland plc v Commission* [1986] ECR 3263, ECJ.
2 Eg Case 27/76 *United Brands v Commission* (Bananas) [1978] ECR 207; Joined Cases 100–103/80 *Musique Diffusion Française SA v Commission* ('the Pioneer case') [1983] ECR 1825, ECJ; Case 107/82 *AEG v Commission* [1983] ECR 3151, ECJ; and Case 322/81 *Michelin v Commission* [1983] ECR 3461, ECJ.
3 Case 243/83 *Binon v AMP* [1985] ECR 2015, ECJ.
4 Under Article 172 regulations made by the Council may give the ECJ 'unlimited jurisdiction in regard to the penalties provided for in such regulations'.
5 EEC Council Regulation 17: First Regulation implementing Articles 85 and 86 of the Treaty (OJ English Special Edition 1959–1962, p 87), see especially Article 17.

Article 3(2) of the Decision provides that, where the same person brings an action before the CFI under one of the first three heads of jurisdiction and an action under Article 40 of the ECSC Treaty, Article 178 of the EEC Treaty or Article 151 of the Euratom Treaty for compensation for damage caused by a Community institution through the act or failure to act which is the subject of the first action, the CFI also has jurisdiction over the damages action. In addition, Article 4 of the Decision gives the CFI jurisdiction over damages actions under Article 34 of the ECSC Treaty,[6] which requires the Commission to compensate undertakings if they have suffered direct and special harm by reason of a decision or recommendation of the Commission which has been annulled and found to involve a fault of such a nature as to render the Community liable. The CFI has not been given jurisdiction over any other damages actions brought by natural or legal persons. The present head of jurisdiction is all the more narrow as damages actions in staff cases will not normally be covered by it but fall under the first head of jurisdiction of the CFI,[7] as being disputes of a financial character within the meaning of Article 91 of the Staff Regulations.

The non-contractual liability of the Communities provided for in Article 40 of the ECSC Treaty, Article 178 of the EEC Treaty and Article 151 of the Euratom Treaty is governed by 'the general principles common to the laws of the Member States'.[8] The ECJ has built up a body of case-law defining what it considers those general principles to be. There are three basic elements of liability: first there must be a wrongful[9] act or omission on the part of the Community; secondly, the applicant must have suffered damage; and thirdly, the damage must have been caused by the Community's act or omission. In addition, the ECJ has imposed stringent conditions for liability to arise in respect of legislative measures: it has consistently held that the Community does not incur liability in respect of a legislative measure which involves choices of economic policy unless a sufficiently serious breach of a superior rule of law for the protection of the individual has occurred.[10] The CFI may build upon this body of case-law and, in so far as it is dealing largely with individual measures, it may have occasion to move away from the more stringent limitations which the ECJ has placed upon liability for general legislative measures.

There is no *locus standi* requirement on the applicant in an action

6 Which has no counterpart in the other two Treaties.
7 Decision, Article 3(1)(a).
8 EEC Treaty, Article 215, second paragraph; Euratom Treaty, Article 188, second paragraph.
9 The ECJ has not so far accepted the principle of liability without fault.
10 See eg Joined Cases 83, 94/76 and 4, 15, 40/77 *Bayerische HNL v Council and Commission* [1978] ECR 1209, ECJ and Joined Cases 116, 124/77 *Amylum v Council and Commission* [1979] ECR 3497.

based on non-contractual liability: the difficulty for such an applicant is rather that of fulfilling the substantive conditions just mentioned. The defendant should be the institution whose act or omission is alleged to have given rise to liability.[11] Proceedings against the Community in matters arising from non-contractual liability are barred after a period of five years from the occurrence of the event giving rise to them.[12]

Plea of illegality

Article 4 of the Decision makes applicable to the CFI Article 184 of the EEC Treaty and Article 156 of the Euratom Treaty, which provide in identical terms that, notwithstanding the expiry of the time-limit laid down for an action for annulment, any party may, in proceedings in which a regulation of the Council or the Commission is in issue, plead the grounds available in annulment actions in order to invoke the inapplicability of that regulation. Article 4 of the Decision also makes applicable to the CFI the third paragraph of Article 36 of the ECSC Treaty which, within a narrower ambit, provides that in appeals against pecuniary sanctions imposed under the ECSC Treaty a party may, under the same conditions as in an action for annulment, contest the legality of the decision or recommendation which that party is alleged not to have observed. Those provisions give the CFI jurisdiction to entertain a 'plea of illegality'.

The plea of illegality does not provide an independent cause of action but may only be invoked where proceedings already lie before the CFI under some other provision.[13] It gives expression to a general principle that a person who is permitted to challenge an individual act may at the same time contest the legality of the general legislation on which the individual act was based and which he is not permitted to challenge directly, eg because of restrictions on locus standi or the expiry of a time-limit.[14] Persons making a plea of illegality may plead any of the four grounds which can found an action for annulment.[15] If successful, such a plea does not lead to the annulment of the general

11 See, before the ECJ, Joined Cases 63–69/72 *Werhahn v Council* [1973] ECR 1229.
12 ECSC Statute, Article 40, applied to the CFI by idem, Article 46; EEC Statute, Article 43, applied to the CFI by idem, Article 46; Euratom Statute, Article 44, applied to the CFI by idem, Article 47.
13 See, before the ECJ, Joined Cases 31, 33/62 *Wöhrmann v Commission* [1962] ECR 501 and Case 21/64 *Macchiorlati Dalmas v High Authority* [1965] ECR 175, ECJ.
14 See, before the ECJ, Case 9/56 *Meroni v High Authority* [1957–58] ECR 133 and Case 92/78 *Simmenthal v Commission* [1979] ECR 777, ECJ.
15 Ie lack of competence, infringement of an essential procedural requirement, infringement of the Treaty or any rule of law relating to its application, or misuse of powers.

measure in question but to a finding that it is inapplicable in the particular case, with the effect that the individual act based on it is deprived of any legal foundation and may be set aside.[16]

Interim relief

Article 4 of the Decision also makes applicable to the CFI the Treaty provisions conferring jurisdiction to suspend the application of an act contested in proceedings before it,[17] to prescribe any necessary interim measures in any case before it[18] and to suspend the enforcement of judgments of the CFI or of decisions of the Council or of the Commission which impose a pecuniary obligation on persons other than States.[19] The power to grant interim measures is extremely important in the categories of case within the jurisdiction of the CFI, which may involve in particular major financial and commercial interests.

The remedy is in the discretion of the CFI. The CFI may suspend the application of an act contested in proceedings before it if it considers that circumstances so require,[20] and it may prescribe any interim measures in any case before it if it considers them necessary.[1] However, the interim measures ordered must be provisional and must in no way prejudice the decision of the CFI on the substance of the case.[2]

The Treaties provide that the President of the CFI may adjudicate upon applications for interim relief by way of summary procedure to be laid down in the Rules of Procedure.[3] The Rules of Procedure

16 That follows from the express terms of Article 184 of the EEC Treaty and Article 156 of the Euratom Treaty, which specify that the plea concerns 'the inapplicability' of the general measure in question. Under the ECSC Treaty no express provision is made but the position is similar: see, before the ECJ, *Meroni* and *Wöhrmann*, cited in footnotes 13 and 14 above.

17 ECSC Treaty, Article 39, second paragraph; EEC Treaty, Article 185; Euratom Treaty, Article 157.

18 ECSC Treaty, Article 39, third paragraph; EEC Treaty, Article 186; Euratom Treaty, Article 158.

19 ECSC Treaty, Articles 44 and 92, third paragraph; EEC Treaty, Articles 187 and 192, fourth paragraph; Euratom Treaty, Articles 159 and 164, third paragraph.

20 ECSC Treaty, Article 39, second paragraph; EEC Treaty, Article 185; Euratom Treaty, Article 157.

 1 ECSC Treaty, Article 39, third paragraph; EEC Treaty, Article 186; Euratom Treaty, Article 158.

 2 ECSC Statute, Article 33, third paragraph, applied to the CFI by idem, Article 46; EEC Statute, Article 36, third paragraph, applied to the CFI by idem, Article 46; Euratom Statute, Article 37, third paragraph, applied to the CFI by idem, Article 47; see also ECJ Rules of Procedure, Article 86(4).

 3 ECSC Statute, Article 33, first paragraph, applied to the CFI by idem, Article 46; EEC Statute, Article 36, first paragraph, applied to the CFI by idem, Article 46; Euratom Statute, Article 37, first paragraph, applied to the CFI by idem, Article 47.

applicable to the CFI are for the time being those of the ECJ, applied *mutatis mutandis*.[4] Those Rules indicate that the application for interim measures must state the subject-matter of the dispute, the circumstances giving rise to urgency and the factual and legal grounds establishing a *prima facie* case for the interim measures applied for.[5] In its case-law the ECJ has interpreted urgency as meaning that it should be necessary for the measures to be issued and to take effect before the decision on the substance of the case in order to avoid serious and irreparable damage to the party seeking them;[6] and it has held that a *prima facie* case for relief is made out if the applicant's claim in the main action, both as to admissibility and as to substance, is supported by serious arguments.[7] For the present that case-law remains relevant to the CFI, but the position may evolve somewhat when the CFI adopts its own Rules of Procedure relating to interim relief.

Matters excluded from the jurisdiction of the CFI

There remains a number of areas of jurisdiction which could have been transferred to the CFI under Article 168a of the Treaty but which have been left outside its jurisdiction by the Decision, in particular actions brought by natural or legal persons against Community anti-dumping and anti-subsidy measures. The ECJ proposed that these also should be included in the jurisdiction of the CFI. The ECJ's case load was characterised in the years preceding the establishment of the CFI by large series of cases in the fields of competition[8] and anti-dumping measures,[9] often raising numerous issues. The ECJ wished to see both

---

4 Decision, Article 11, third paragraph.
5 ECJ Rules of Procedure, Article 83(2).
6 See eg Joined Cases 60, 190/81R *IBM v Commission* [1981] ECR 1857, ECJ.
7 See eg Joined Cases 228, 229/82R *Ford v Commission* [1982] ECR 3091, ECJ and Case 269/84R *Fabbro v Commission* [1984] ECR 4333, ECJ.
8 Eg the Woodpulp cases (89/85 *Ahlström v Commission*, 104/85 *Bowater v Commission*, 114/85 *Pulp, Paper and Paperboard Export Association v Commission*, 116/85 *St Anne – Nackawic Pulp and Paper Co v Commission*, 117/85 *International Pulp Sales Co v Commission*, 125/85 *Westar Timber v Commission*, 126/85 *Weldwood of Canada v Commission*, 127/85 *MacMillan Bloedel v Commission*, 128/85 *Canadian Forest Products v Commission* and 129/85 *British Columbia Forest Products v Commission*).
9 Eg the Mini Ball Bearings cases (240/84 *NTN Toyo v Council*, 255/84 *Nachi Fujikoshi v Council*, 256/84 *Koyo Seiko v Council*, 258/84 *Nippon Seiko v Council* and 260/84 *Minebea v Council* [1987] ECR 1809, 1861, 1899, 1923 and 1975) and the Electronic Typewriter cases (56/85 *Brother v Commission*, 250/85 *Brother v Council*, 260/85 and 106/86 *Tokyo Electric Co v Council*, 273/85, 107/86 *Silver Seiko v Council*, 277 and 300/85 *Canon v Council* and 301/85 *Sharp v Council*, all judgments of 5 October 1988).

categories of case transferred to the CFI and confine all the fact-finding activities in such cases to the CFI. As has been seen, the competition cases were transferred, but following opposition from the Commission and France, the Council could not agree to transfer anti-dumping cases to the CFI. By way of a compromise the Council provided, in Article 3(3) of the Decision, that, after two years of operation of the CFI,[10] it would re-examine the ECJ's proposal to give the CFI jurisdiction in relation to measures against dumping and subsidies. The re-examination is to be made 'in the light of experience, including the development of jurisprudence'.[11] It is possible, therefore, that after the two years specified anti-dumping and anti-subsidy cases may be transferred to the CFI, particularly if it is felt that in the meantime the case-law of the ECJ has settled the main questions in the field.

A number of other areas potentially within the jurisdiction of the CFI were not transferred by the Decision because the ECJ did not propose their transfer. They include actions concerning State aids brought by natural or legal persons. The ECJ refrained from proposing the transfer of such actions to the CFI on the basis that they essentially sought to obtain the condemnation of a Commission decision relating to the conduct of a Member State and frequently gave rise to parallel actions by the Member States concerned. It may be thought, however, that the possibility of parallel actions in the two courts is not a serious obstacle to the transfer of this area of jurisdiction to the CFI: it did not for example prevent the transfer of competition cases to the CFI, and procedures to deal with such an event are specifically provided in Article 47 of the Statute. In principle the complex factual questions which such cases regularly involve suit them for hearing by the CFI; but in so far as they indirectly sanction the conduct of Member States, the Council might be reluctant to agree to their transfer.

It would also have been possible to propose the transfer to the CFI of all damages actions brought by natural or legal persons, but the ECJ refrained from doing so and limited its proposal to those damages actions which were linked to annulment actions or actions for failure to act brought by the same person and falling within the jurisdiction of the CFI. It preferred for the time being to retain jurisdiction in the other damages actions in particular because such actions often raise indirectly the issue of the invalidity of a legislative act of general application, a matter which it felt ought rather to be decided by the

10 The Member States agreed that the two years are to run from the date of the publication of the ruling by the President of the ECJ that the CFI has been constituted in accordance with law, ie 31 October 1989: see 'The Essential Minimum: the Establishment of the Court of First Instance' by T Kennedy in *European Law Review* 1989, p 7, footnote 49.
11 'Jurisprudence' here means 'case-law'; cf the French version: *'compte tenu de l'expérience acquise, notamment de l'évolution de la jurisprudence'.*

ECJ. However, the ECJ made it clear in its proposal that that approach was a pragmatic one and that there was no objection of principle to the wider inclusion of actions for damages in the transfer of jurisdiction to the CFI. Moreover it expressly acknowledged that such actions often raise complex questions of fact which would justify a transfer of jurisdiction to the CFI. That is a clear indication that the ECJ may in the future propose a wider transfer of jurisdiction in relation to damages actions.

The ECJ also refrained from proposing the transfer to the CFI of cases brought by natural or legal persons under an arbitration clause, pursuant to Article 181 of the EEC Treaty. In that connection it may be argued that it is desirable to avoid cases of an exactly similar type going to the CFI if brought by the party to the contract who was a natural or legal person but to the ECJ if brought by the party who was a Community institution.[12] However, such an argument does not seem conclusive, as a comparable lack of symmetry between preliminary rulings and direct actions did not prevent the transfer of competition cases to the CFI. Moreover, the litigation involved in disputes under arbitration clauses is of a kind exactly suited to hearing by a first instance court.

Finally, by confining the range of annulment actions to the subject-matter specified in its proposal, the ECJ excluded a relatively small number of miscellaneous annulment actions brought by natural or legal persons. Such actions may concern general legislative measures in relation to which the applicant must establish direct and individual concern.[13] On the other hand they may concern individual measures addressed to a natural or legal person in matters other than those specified in the Decision, such as individual decisions relating to customs matters.[14] The latter type of case, it is submitted, is well suited to be dealt with by the CFI, particularly where it involves evidence on complex scientific or technical questions.

Impact of the transfer of jurisdiction to the CFI

The effect of excluding the above categories of case from transfer to the CFI is illustrated in Tables III and IV. Table III shows the CFI's hypothetical share of the cases brought before the ECJ between 1980

12 Example of the former: Case 220/85 *Fadex NV v Commission* [1986] ECR 3387; example of the latter: Case 426/85 *Commission v Zoubek* [1986] ECR 4057.
13 Eg Case 232/81 *Agricola Commerciale Olio v Commission* [1984] ECR 3881, concerning the annulment of two regulations in the field of agriculture.
14 Eg Case 13/84 *Control Data v Commission* [1987] ECR 275, concerning the annulment of a decision on the duty-free importation of a particular type of computer.

TABLE III – EXTENT OF THE CFI'S JURISDICTON – ILLUSTRATION ON THE BASIS OF CASES BROUGHT BEFORE THE ECJ 1980–1988

	1980	1981	1982	1983	1984	1985	1986	1987	1988	Total
I Cases brought before the ECJ	279	323	345	297	312	433	329	395	373	3,086
II Cases which would have come within the full jurisdiction of the CFI under Articles 32d ECSC, 168a EEC and 140a Euratom	148	157	160	148	119	152	137	158	94	1,273
III Cases which would have come within the jurisdiction of the CFI as defined in the Decision										
Staff Cases	116	94	85	68	43	65	57	77	58	
Coal & Steel Cases	7	32	24	33	29	31	21	24	2	
Competition Cases	6	6	29	7	8	18	17	13	5	
Total	129	132	138	108	80	114	95	114	65	975
IV Cases excluded from the potential jurisdiction of the CFI by the terms of the Decision										
Dumping and Subsidies Cases	–	2	6	3	6	12	13	18	2	
Other Cases	19	23	16	37	33	26	29	26	27	
Total	19	25	22	40	39	38	42	44	29	298

and 1988. On a maximum transfer of jurisdiction, the CFI would have taken over 41% of the ECJ's cases in that period: under the Decision it would have taken over only 32%. The terms of the Decision would have excluded from transfer roughly a quarter of the cases which could have been transferred to the CFI on a maximum transfer of jurisdiction.

Turning to the cases which actually fell to be transferred from the ECJ to the CFI on 31 October 1989, Table IV shows that, of the cases then pending before the ECJ, 24% were actually transferred to the CFI whereas 33% could have been transferred on a maximum transfer of jurisdiction. The terms of the Decision excluded roughly a quarter of the potentially transferable cases from being transferred to the CFI.

TABLE IV – TRANSFER OF JURISDICTION IN PENDING CASES AS AT
31 OCTOBER 1989*

I	Cases pending before the ECJ immediately before the transfer of jurisdiction		622
II	Pending cases to be transfered to the CFI under the terms of the Decision		
	Staff Cases	76	
	Coal & Steel Cases	2	
	Competition Cases	73	
	Total		151
III	Pending cases excluded from transfer to the CFI by the terms of the Decision		
	Dumping & Subsidy Cases	22	
	State Aid Cases	4	
	Cases under an Arbitration Clause	2	
	Other Cases	31	
	Total		59
IV	Cases left pending before the ECJ immediately after the transfer of jurisdiction		471

* The cases were in fact transferred by orders adopted on 15 November 1989. Because of events which occurred between the two dates, the number of cases actually transferred to the CFI was slightly smaller than the number which fell to be transferred on 31 October 1989.

It also emerges from Table IV that the establishment of the CFI relieved the ECJ of only 151 cases and left 471 cases still pending before it. While that is a substantial reduction, it is only a quarter of the ECJ's backlog. In order to eliminate it, further steps will be needed. One possible step is an extension of the jurisdiction of the CFI to include some or all of the categories not covered by the Decision. The ECJ has left open the possibility of widening the CFI's jurisdiction, and there are, it is submitted, reasons for transferring to the CFI all the categories of case currently excluded from its jurisdiction. Taking that possibility along with the review of anti-dumping and anti-subsidy jurisdiction provided for in Article 3(3) of the Decision, there are prospects that the jurisdiction of the CFI may be widened in the future. However, the scope of the jurisdiction of the CFI will in any event continue to remain limited by the terms of Article 168a of the Treaty.

Finally, it may be observed that the cases which fell to be transferred to the CFI when it started operation on 31 October 1989 were divided evenly between staff cases and 'economic law' cases. While it is not possible to foretell the future trend of litigation, it is interesting to note the even balance existing at the outset between the two main types of case coming before the CFI, as it will affect the working of the CFI and in particular the arrangements regarding its chambers.

4 Procedure before the CFI

The legislative framework

The main points of the procedure before the CFI are laid down in the Statute. The second sentence of Article 168a(2) of the Treaty provides that, unless the Council decides otherwise, the provisions of the Treaty relating to the ECJ, in particular the provisions of the Statute, shall apply to the CFI. Far from 'deciding otherwise', in its Decision establishing the CFI the Council expressly provided that the procedure before the CFI was to be governed by Title III of the Statute ('Procedure'), with the exception of those of its articles which concerned proceedings outside the jurisdiction of the CFI.[1] The application of Title III of the Statute to the CFI was modified in only one respect, namely the requirement of the 'hearing' of the Advocate General's Opinion.[2] It was provided that, notwithstanding that requirement, an Advocate General in the CFI could deliver his Opinion in writing.[3] The Decision also added two further articles concerning procedure before the CFI to the Statute as part of the new Title IV of the Statute ('The CFI').[4]

1 The first paragraph of Article 46 of the ECSC Statute, inserted by the Decision, provides that the procedure before the CFI shall be governed by Title III of the ECSC Statute (Articles 20 to 43) with the exception of Articles 41 and 42, which relate to disputes between Member States under Article 89 of the ECSC Treaty. The first paragraph of Article 46 of the EEC Statute, inserted by the Decision, provides that the procedure before the CFI shall be governed by Title III of the EEC Statute (Articles 17 to 43) with the exception of Article 20, which concerns preliminary rulings. The first paragraph of Article 47 of the Euratom Statute, inserted by the Decision, provides that the procedure before the CFI shall be governed by Title III of the Euratom Statute (Articles 17 to 44) with the exception of Articles 20 and 21, which concern, respectively, appeals against decisions of the Arbitration Commitee under Article 18 of the Euratom Treaty and preliminary rulings.
2 ECSC Statute, Article 21, fourth paragraph; EEC Statute, Article 18, fourth paragraph; Euratom Statute, Article 18, fourth paragraph.
3 ECSC Statute, Article 46, third paragraph; EEC Statute, Article 46, third paragraph; Euratom Statute, Article 47, third paragraph.
4 Article 47 relating to conflicts of jurisdiction between the CFI and the ECJ and Article 48 on notification of certain decisions of the CFI; see below under 'Outline of Procedure before the CFI'.

For the rest, such further and more detailed provisions as may be necessary are to be laid down in the Rules of Procedure of the CFI.[5] The CFI is under an obligation to establish its Rules of Procedure[6] and to do so immediately upon its constitution.[7] However, the process of adopting those Rules of Procedure takes a certain amount of time and, at the time of writing, had not yet been completed. It is provided that, until the entry into force of the Rules of Procedure of the CFI, the Rules of Procedure of the ECJ shall apply *mutatis mutandis*.[8]

It is clear that certain questions as to the procedure of the CFI cannot be resolved by the Rules of Procedure of the ECJ, even applied *mutatis mutandis*: in particular, the arrangements regarding the hearing of cases in chambers and in plenary session and the arrangements for an Advocate General to deliver an Opinion in certain cases before the CFI. None the less, the ECJ's Rules of Procedure contain provisions governing most aspects of procedure before the CFI, including in particular preparatory enquiries.[9] Thus in the initial period of its operation, the CFI will be applying the ECJ's Rules of Procedure, where necessary *mutatis mutandis*; and in relation to the few points not governed by those Rules, it is anticipated that the CFI will, of necessity, take *ad hoc* decisions pending the adoption of its own Rules of Procedure.

In sum, during the initial period of its operation, procedure before the CFI will be governed almost entirely by the same rules as procedure before the ECJ, that is Title III of the Statute and the ECJ's Rules of Procedure. Moreover, even when the CFI's Rules of Procedure are adopted, it seems unlikely that they will differ radically from the ECJ's Rules of Procedure because, like them, they are restricted to supplementing the basic procedural rules already contained in the Statute.

---

5 Statute, Article 46, second paragraph.
6 EEC Treaty, Article 168a(4).
7 Decision, Article 11, second paragraph.
8 Decision, Article 11, third paragraph. The Rules of Procedure of the ECJ applicable to the CFI are reproduced in Appendix IV below.
  The Decision does not mention the Supplementary Rules adopted by the ECJ pursuant to Article 111 of its Rules of Procedure concerning its practice in relation to (a) letters rogatory, (b) applications for legal aid and (c) reports of perjury by witnesses or experts, as adopted on 4 December 1974 (OJ 1974 L 350, p 29) and amended on 16 September 1981 (OJ 1981 L 282, p 1) and 8 May 1987 (OJ 1987 L 165, p 4). In the absence of any express provision to that effect, it is thought that the Supplementary Rules do not apply to the CFI.
9 ECJ Rules of Procedure, Articles 45 to 54.

Outline of procedure before the CFI

General matters

The establishment of the CFI, alongside the ECJ, made it necessary to make provisions for the problems arising from cases brought before the CFI but concerning the ECJ, and vice versa. That was the object of Article 47 of the Statute.[10] In Article 47, three situations are envisaged. First, where a procedural document is plainly lodged by mistake in the wrong Registry, the first paragraph of Article 47 provides that that Registry simply transmits it 'immediately' to the right Registry. The use of the word 'immediately' seems to indicate that in these circumstances time does not run against the party concerned. Secondly, if either court finds that it does not have jurisdiction over a case brought before it, the second paragraph of Article 47 provides that it refers the case to the other court; but the process cannot go on indefinitely as the ECJ's reference is final.[11] Thirdly, where each court has jurisdiction over a case but the cases raise the same issue, the third paragraph of Article 47 provides a choice of solutions. Where cases before the CFI and before the ECJ each raise the same issue, the CFI 'may after hearing the parties' stay its proceedings until the ECJ has delivered judgment. Where parallel cases seek the annulment of the same art, the CFI may not merely stay its proceedings but refer the case pending before it to the ECJ for judgment.[12] Conversely, the ECJ may stay proceedings in a parallel case pending before it, in which event the proceedings before the CFI must continue. The powers conferred by the third paragraph of Article 47 are inspired by a concern for uniformity of the case-law and economy of procedure, as well as by a concern that suspension of proceedings before the CFI should not deprive a party of its right to be heard.

Parties other than a Member State or a Community institution must be represented by a lawyer entitled to practise before a court of a Member State.[13] Member States and Community institutions, on the other hand, must be represented by an agent who need not be legally qualified but who may be assisted by an adviser or by a lawyer entitled to practise before a court of a Member State.[14] University teachers who are nationals of a Member State whose law gives them a right of

10 Which was inserted in the Statute along with the other articles of Title IV thereof by the Decision establishing the CFI.
11 This provision, along with the provision in Article 51 of the Statute for appeals to lie on grounds of lack of competence of the CFI, ensures that the ECJ has the last word on the interpretation of the rules defining the jurisdiction of the CFI.
12 The words used in Article 47 are that the CFI 'may decline jurisdiction in order that the Court of Justice may rule on such applications'.
13 Statute, Article 17, second paragraph.
14 Statute, Article 17, first paragraph.

audience may act before the CFI as lawyers entitled to practise before a court of a Member State.[15] At the hearing a party may address the CFI only through his agent, adviser or lawyer.[16] The privileges and immunities, rights and obligations of agents, advisers and lawyers appearing before the CFI are laid down in Articles 32 to 36 of the ECJ's Rules of Procedure.

A party who is wholly or in part unable to meet the costs of the proceedings before the CFI may at any time apply for legal aid.[17] The application, which need not be made through a lawyer,[18] must be accompanied by evidence of the applicant's need of assistance and in particular by a document from the competent authority certifying his lack of means.[19] When the application for legal aid has been lodged, the President of the CFI designates a judge to act as Rapporteur, and the Chamber of which that judge is a member considers the application and decides whether legal aid should be granted in full or in part.[20] [1] The Chamber makes an order without giving reasons, and no appeal lies from it.[2]

The language of a case must be Danish, Dutch, English, French, German, Greek, Irish, Italian, Portuguese or Spanish.[3] The language of a case is chosen by the applicant.[4] It must in particular be used in the parties' written pleadings and oral addresses to the CFI, in supporting documents and in the decisions of the CFI.[5] Supporting documents expressed in a language other than the language of the case must be accompanied by a translation into that language,[6] but in the case of long documents translations may be confined to extracts.[7] By way of exception to the general rules, the CFI may authorise another of the above languages to be used as the language of the case for all or part of the proceedings either at the joint request of the parties[8] or at the request of one of the parties subject to hearing the opposite party.[9] If a

15 Statute, Article 17, fifth paragraph.
16 Statute, Article 18, fourth paragraph, and Article 29.
17 ECJ Rules of Procedure, Article 76(1).
18 ECJ Rules of Procedure, Article 76(2), second sub-paragraph.
19 ECJ Rules of Procedure, Article 76(1), second sub-paragraph.
20 ECJ Rules of Procedure, Article 76(3), first sub-paragraph.
 1 As to the criteria applied by the ECJ in awarding legal aid, see 'Paying the Pip'
    Legal Aid in Proceedings before the Court of Justice', Tom Kennedy, 1988 *Comm.*
    Market Law Review, p 559.
 2 ECJ Rules of Procedure, Article 76(3), second sub-paragraph; see also Statute,
    Articles 49 to 51.
 3 ECJ Rules of Procedure, Article 29(1).
 4 ECJ Rules of Procedure, Article 29(2).
 5 ECJ Rules of Procedure, Article 29(3), first sub-paragraph.
 6 ECJ Rules of Procedure, Article 29(3), second sub-paragraph.
 7 ECJ Rules of Procedure, Article 29(3), third sub-paragraph.
 8 ECJ Rules of Procedure, Article 29(2)(b).
 9 ECJ Rules of Procedure, Article 29(2)(c). Such a request may not be submitted by a
    Community institution.

Member State intervenes in proceedings before the CFI it is entitled to use its official language both in written pleadings and oral addresses to the CFI.[10] A procedural language other than the language of the case may be used by the President of the CFI or the President of a Chamber when conducting oral proceedings, by Members of the CFI in putting questions and by Advocates General in delivering their Opinions, if any.[11] Where a Member State or a Member of the CFI uses a language other than the language of the case, the Registrar arranges for translation into the language of the case.[12]

The time-limits within which proceedings must be commenced before the CFI are defined in the relevant provision establishing the jurisdiction.[13] However, no right may be prejudiced in consequence of the expiry of a time-limit if the party concerned proves the existence of unforeseeable circumstances or of *force majeure*.[14] The period of time allowed for commencing proceedings against a measure adopted by a Community institution runs from the day following the receipt by the person concerned of notification of the measure or, where the measure is published, from the fifteenth day after its publication in the Official Journal of the European Communities.[15] In addition, extensions to the prescribed time-limits are granted in order to take account of distance from the CFI.[16] In reckoning any period of time prescribed by the Treaty, the Statute or the ECJ's Rules of Procedure for the taking of any procedural step, the day of the event from which the period is to run is excluded, and time continues to run during the vacations.[17] If the period would otherwise end on a Sunday or an official holiday it is extended until the end of the first following working day.[18] Any time-limit prescribed pursuant to the ECJ's Rules of Procedure (but not any other instrument) may be extended by whoever prescribed it.[19]

---

10 ECJ Rules of Procedure, Article 29(3), fourth sub-paragraph.
11 ECJ Rules of Procedure, Article 29(5).
12 ECJ Rules of Procedure, Article 29(3), fourth sub-paragraph, and (5).
13 See, eg the third paragraph of Article 173 of the EEC Treaty, establishing the two-month time-limit for the bringing of an annulment action under that Treaty.
14 Statute, Article 42, second paragraph.
15 ECJ Rules of Procedure, Article 81(1).
16 Statute, Article 42, first paragraph; ECJ Rules of Procedure, Article 81(2) and Annex II. The extensions, for all parties save those habitually resident in Luxembourg, are: for Belgium, two days; for the Federal Republic of Germany and the European territories of France and the Netherlands, six days; for the European territory of Denmark, and for Greece, Ireland, Italy, Spain, Portugal (except for the Azores and Madeira) and the United Kingdom, ten days; for other European countries and territories, two weeks; for the Azores and Madeira, three weeks; and for other countries, departments and territories, one month.
17 ECJ Rules of Procedure, Article 80(1).
18 ECJ Rules of Procedure, Article 80(2), first sub-paragraph.
19 ECJ Rules of Procedure, Article 82.

The normal stages of procedure

The procedure before the CFI consists of two parts: written and oral.[20] The written procedure comprises the communication of the various written pleadings and supporting documents.[1] After the close of the written pleadings, the CFI considers whether to undertake a preparatory enquiry or any other preparatory step.[2] The oral procedure then consists of the reading of the Judge-Rapporteur's Report for the Hearing,[3] the hearing, if any, of witnesses and experts, the hearing by the CFI of agents, advisers and lawyers and the hearing of the Advocate General's Opinion, if any.[4] After the close of the oral procedure, the CFI proceeds to judgment.

Proceedings are commenced by lodging a written application at the Registry of the CFI.[5] The original of every pleading must be signed by the party's agent or lawyer and bear a date.[6] A file containing the supporting documents and a schedule listing them must be annexed to the pleading.[7] The original of the pleading, accompanied by all annexes referred to in it, must be lodged at the CFI together with five copies for the CFI and one copy for every other party to the proceedings.[8] The application must state: the name and permanent address of the applicant; the name of the party against whom the application is made; the subject-matter of the dispute and the grounds on which the application is based; the form of order sought by the applicant; and the nature of any evidence relied upon by him.[9] The application must state an address for service in Luxembourg and the name of a person who is authorised and willing to accept service.[10] The lawyer acting for a party must lodge at the Registry of the CFI a certificate that he is entitled to practise before a court of a Member State.[11] In actions for annulment or actions for failure to act, the application must be accompanied by the measure of which annulment is sought or by documentary evidence of the date on which the defendant was requested to act.[12] Applications made by a legal person governed by private law must be accompanied by the instrument

20 Statute, Article 18, first paragraph.
 1 Statute, Article 18, second paragraph.
 2 ECJ Rules of Procedure, Article 44(1).
 3 In practice before the ECJ the Report for the Hearing is not read out but simply taken as read.
 4 Statute, Article 18, fourth paragraph.
 5 Statute, Article 19, first paragraph.
 6 ECJ Rules of Procedure, Article 37(1) and (3).
 7 ECJ Rules of Procedure, Article 37(4).
 8 ECJ Rules of Procedure, Article 37(1).
 9 Statute, Article 19, first paragraph; ECJ Rules of Procedure, Article 38(1).
10 ECJ Rules of Procedure, Article 38(2).
11 ECJ Rules of Procedure, Article 38(3).
12 Statute, Article 19, second paragraph; ECJ Rules of Procedure, Article 38(4).

constituting that legal person and proof that the authority granted to the applicant's lawyer has been properly conferred on him by someone authorised for the purpose.[13] If an application does not comply with the requirement to state an address for service and the name of a person authorised to accept service and with the requirements relating to the documents which must accompany the application, the Registrar of the CFI prescribes a reasonable period within which the applicant is to comply with those requirements, failing which the CFI may reject the application on the ground of want of form.[14]

When proceedings are commenced, notice of the fact is given in the Official Journal of the European Communities. The notice comprises the date when the application originating proceedings was lodged at the Registry of the CFI, the names and permanent residences of the parties, the subject-matter of the dispute, the claims made in the application and a summary of the contentions and main arguments adduced in support.[15]

The service of written pleadings on the other parties is the responsibility of the Registrar of the CFI, not of the parties themselves.[16] In particular, the Registrar arranges for the application to be served on the defendant.[17] Service is effected either by personal delivery of a copy of the document at the address for service of the person concerned or by sending a copy by registered post with a form for acknowledgement of receipt.[18]

Within one month of service on him of the application, the defendant must lodge a defence.[19] That time-limit may be extended by the President of the CFI on a reasoned application by the defendant.[20] A defence must state: the name and permanent residence of the defendant; the points of fact and law relied on; the form of order sought; the nature of any evidence relied on;[1] and an address for service in Luxembourg and the name of a person authorised and willing to accept service.[2] The documents required to accompany a defence are the same as those required in the case of an application.[3]

---

13 ECJ Rules of Procedure, Article 38(5).
14 ECJ Rules of Procedure, Article 38(7).
15 ECJ Rules of Procedure, Article 16(6).
16 ECJ Rules of Procedure, Article 17(1); see also Statute, Article 18, third paragraph.
17 ECJ Rules of Procedure, Article 39.
18 ECJ Rules of Procedure, Article 79(1).
19 ECJ Rules of Procedure, Article 40(1).
20 ECJ Rules of Procedure, Article 40(2).
 1 ECJ Rules of Procedure, Article 40(1), first sub-paragraph.
 2 ECJ Rules of Procedure, Article 38(2), applied by *idem* Article 40(1), second sub-paragraph.
 3 ECJ Rules of Procedure, Article 38(3) to (5), applied by *idem* Article 40(1), second sub-paragraph.

The application and the defence may be supplemented by a reply from the applicant and a rejoinder from the defendant.[4] The President of the CFI fixes the time-limits within which those pleadings are to be lodged.[5] In a reply or rejoinder, a party may indicate further evidence as long as he gives reasons for the delay in indicating it,[6] but no fresh issue may be raised unless it is based on matters of law or of fact which came to light in the course of the written procedure.[7] If a fresh issue is so raised, the President of the CFI may allow the other party time to answer,[8] and the decision on admissibility is reserved for the final judgment.[9]

After the rejoinder has been lodged (or where no reply or no rejoinder has been lodged within the time-limit fixed or where the party concerned waives his right to lodge a reply or rejoinder) the President of the CFI fixes a date on which the Judge-Rapporteur[10] is to present a preliminary report to the CFI.[11] The report contains recommendations as to whether a preparatory enquiry or other preparatory step should be undertaken and as to the appropriate formation to hear the case. It is for the CFI to decide what action to take upon the recommendations of the Judge-Rapporteur.[12]

The CFI is normally required to sit in Chambers of three or five judges. It may, however, sit in plenary session in certain cases governed by its Rules of Procedure.[13] The composition of the Chambers and the assignment of cases to them is to be governed by the CFI's Rules of Procedure.[14] Pending the adoption of the CFI's Rules of Procedure, the ECJ's Rules of Procedure apply *mutatis mutandis*, but they do not provide a complete body of rules for this area.[15] It is clear from the ECJ's Rules that the CFI must decide which judges shall be attached to its Chambers, appoint Presidents of the Chambers, and

4 ECJ Rules of Procedure, Article 41(1).
5 ECJ Rules of Procedure, Article 41(2).
6 ECJ Rules of Procedure, Article 42(1).
7 ECJ Rules of Procedure, Article 42(2), first sub-paragraph.
8 ECJ Rules of Procedure, Article 42(2), second sub-paragraph.
9 ECJ Rules of Procedure, Article 42(2), third sub-paragraph.
10 As soon as an application originating proceedings has been lodged, the President of the CFI designates a judge to act as Rapporteur in the case: ECJ Rules of Procedure, Article 9(2).
11 The preliminary report is presented only to the CFI and is not a public document.
12 ECJ Rules of Procedure, Article 44(1); see also *idem*, Article 95(2), first sub-paragraph.
13 Decision, Article 2(4). This is the converse of the rule governing the ECJ, which must normally sit in plenary session but may form Chambers of three or five judges either to undertake certain preparatory enquiries or to adjudicate on particular categories of cases in accordance with rules laid down for those purposes: ECSC Treaty, Article 32, second paragraph; EEC Treaty, Article 165, second paragraph; and Euratom Treaty, Article 137, second paragraph.
14 Decision, Article 2(4).
15 See ECJ Rules of Procedure, Articles 9, 10(1), 95 and 96.

publish the composition of the Chambers in the Official Journal of the European Communities.[16] It has accordingly set up two Chambers of five judges and three Chambers of three judges.[17] It is also clear that the Rules of Procedure applying to proceedings before the plenary formation apply in corresponding manner to the proceedings before the Chambers and that, in proceedings before a Chamber, the powers of the President of the CFI are exercised by the President of the Chamber.[18] The ECJ's Rules of Procedure also indicate that staff cases as a general rule must be tried by a Chamber,[19] and all other categories of case within the jurisdiction of the CFI may be tried by a Chamber.[20] It seems that a case may not be assigned to a Chamber if a Member State or Community institution which is a party or an intervener in the proceedings has requested that the case be decided in plenary session.[1] Furthermore, it appears that a Chamber may at any stage refer to the plenary formation any case assigned to or devolving upon it.[2] However, the extent to which those rules can be applied to the CFI is uncertain. At the time of writing the cases which may be heard in plenary session and the principles governing the assignment of cases to Chambers remain to be elaborated in the CFI's Rules of Procedure. However, for its first year of operation, the CFI decided on 4 October 1989 to assign staff cases to the three-judge Chambers and other cases to the five-judge Chambers in turn according to the order in which they are registered, save that the President of the CFI may decide otherwise on the ground that cases are related or with a view to ensuring an even spread of the workload between the Chambers.[3]

Measures of enquiry may be undertaken by the CFI itself or assigned to a Chamber or to the Judge-Rapporteur.[4] The CFI prescribes the measures of enquiry that it considers appropriate by an order setting out the issues of fact to be determined, and the order is served on the parties.[5] The Advocate General, if there is one in the case, takes part in the measures of enquiry[6] and the parties are entitled to attend them.[7] Evidence may be submitted in rebuttal and previous evidence may be

---

16 ECJ Rules of Procedure, Articles 9(1) and 10(1).
17 See OJ 1989 C 281, p 12.
18 ECJ Rules of Procedure, Article 9(4).
19 ECJ Rules of Procedure, Article 95(3).
20 ECJ Rules of Procedure, Article 95(1).
 1 ECJ Rules of Procedure, Article 95(2), second sub-paragraph.
 2 ECJ Rules of Procedure, Article 95(4).
 3 OJ 1989 C 281, p 13.
 4 ECJ Rules of Procedure, Article 44(2), first sub-paragraph, Article 45(3), first sub-paragraph, and Article 60.
 5 ECJ Rules of Procedure, Article 45(1).
 6 ECJ Rules of Procedure, Article 45(3), second sub-paragraph.
 7 ECJ Rules of Procedure, Article 46(3).

amplified.[8] After the preparatory enquiry has been completed, the parties may be given an opportunity to lodge written observations.[9]

The range of measures of enquiry within the power of the CFI is broad. Under the Statute it is entitled to require the parties to produce all documents and to supply all information which it considers desirable. Formal note is taken of any refusal. It may also require the Member States and institutions not parties to the case to supply all information which it considers necessary for the proceedings.[10] Furthermore the CFI may at any time entrust any individual, body, authority, committee or other organisation it chooses with the task of giving an expert opinion.[11] Without prejudice to those powers, the ECJ's Rules of Procedure provide that the following measures of enquiry may be adopted: (a) the personal appearance of the parties; (b) a request for information and production of documents; (c) oral testimony; (d) experts' reports; and (e) an inspection of the place or thing in question.[12] As regards oral testimony, detailed provision is made for the summoning and examination of witnesses and experts in Articles 47 to 53 of the ECJ's Rules of Procedure.[13]

In this connection, mention should also be made of Article 23 of the ECSC Statute.[14] Under that provision, 'where proceedings are instituted against a decision of one of the institutions of the Community, that institution shall transmit to the Court all the documents relating to the case before the Court'. That far-reaching disclosure provision has no counterpart in either the EEC or the Euratom Statutes. Furthermore, in the field of staff cases, Article 26 of the Staff Regulations provides that an official's personal file, which is otherwise confidential, must be forwarded to the ECJ if an action concerning the official is brought before the ECJ. It is thought that that provision now falls to be interpreted as extending to the CFI.

The President of the CFI fixes the date for the opening of the oral

---

8 ECJ Rules of Procedure, Article 45(4).
9 ECJ Rules of Procedure, Article 54.
10 EEC Statute, Article 21; Euratom Statute, Article 22. Article 24 of the ECSC Statute provides: 'The Court may require the parties, their representatives or agents or the Governments of the Member States to produce all documents and to supply all information which the Court considers desirable. Formal note shall be taken of any refusal'.
11 EEC Statute, Article 22; Euratom Statute, Article 23. Article 25 of the ECSC Statute provides: 'The Court may at any time entrust any individual, body, authority, committee or other organisation it chooses with the task of holding an enquiry or giving an expert opinion; to this end it may compile a list of individuals or bodies approved as experts'.
12 ECJ Rules of Procedure, Article 45(2).
13 See also ECSC Statute, Article 28; EEC Statute, Articles 23 to 27; and Euratom Statute, Articles 24 to 28.
14 Applicable to the CFI by virtue of ECSC Statute, Article 46, first paragraph.

procedure after the preparatory enquiry has been completed.[15] The CFI may also decide to open the oral procedure without ordering any preparatory enquiry, in which case the President of the CFI fixes a date for the opening of the oral procedure after the close of the written procedure.[16] The two main components of the oral procedure are the hearing of the parties through their agents, advisers or lawyers and the hearing of the Advocate General's Opinion. In the CFI, however, an Advocate General's Opinion is not necessarily delivered in every case and the criteria for selecting the cases in which an Opinion is to be delivered have yet to be laid down in the Rules of Procedure of the CFI.[17]

The hearing of a case before the CFI is held in public unless for serious reasons the CFI decides otherwise.[18] The oral proceedings in cases which are held *in camera* are not published.[19] The proceedings are opened and directed by the President of the CFI or by the President of the Chamber, as the case may be,[20] who is responsible for the proper conduct of the hearing.[1] A party may address the CFI only through his agent, adviser or lawyer;[2] but during the hearing the President of the CFI, the other judges and the Advocate General if there is one, may put questions to the agents, advisers or lawyers of the parties[3] and may examine the experts and witnesses, if any, and the parties themselves.[4]

Where an Advocate General's Opinion falls to be delivered in a case before the CFI, it is delivered after the parties have been heard, at the end of the oral procedure,[5] but in the CFI the Advocate General may deliver his Opinion in writing.[6] An Opinion must be impartial, independent and fully reasoned; it is designed to assist the CFI in reaching its decision but is not binding.[7] After the Opinion, if any, has been delivered, the President of the CFI declares the oral procedure closed.[8]

The plenary CFI or the Chamber, as the case may be, deliberates on

---

15 ECJ Rules of Procedure, Article 54.
16 ECJ Rules of Procedure, Article 44(2), second sub-paragraph.
17 Decision, Article 2(3).
18 Statute, Article 28.
19 ECJ Rules of Procedure, Article 56(2).
20 ECJ Rules of Procedure, Article 9(4).
 1 ECJ Rules of Procedure, Article 56(1).
 2 Statute, Article 29; ECJ Rules of Procedure, Article 58.
 3 ECJ Rules of Procedure, Article 57.
 4 Statute, Article 29.
 5 Statute, Article 18, fourth paragraph; ECJ Rules of Procedure, Article 59(1).
 6 Statute, Article 46, third paragraph.
 7 Decision, Article 2(3), second sub-paragraph. Similar conditions apply to the Opinion of the Advocate General before the ECJ: Treaty, Article 166, second paragraph.
 8 ECJ Rules of Procedure, Article 59(2).

its judgment in secret[9] and in the absence of the Advocate General, if one has been appointed in the case.[10] The original of the judgment is signed by the President of the CFI, the judges who took part in the deliberations and the Registrar.[11] No provision is made for dissenting judgments. The judgment contains: a statement that it is the judgement of the CFI; the date of its delivery; the names of the Presidents and the judges taking part in it; the name of the Advocate General, if any; the name of the Registrar; the description of the parties; the names of the agents, advisers and lawyers of the parties; the submissions of the parties; a statement, where appropriate, that the Advocate General has been heard; a summary of the facts; the grounds for the decision; and the operative part of the judgment, including the decision as to costs.[12]

The judgment is delivered in open court, and the parties are given notice to attend to hear it.[13] The parties are also served with certified copies of the judgment.[14] Moreover, final decisions of the CFI, decisions disposing of the substantive issues in part only, or disposing of a procedural issue concerning a plea of lack of competence or inadmissibility (ie the decisions subject to appeal before the ECJ pursuant to Article 49 of the Statute) are notified by the Registrar of the CFI not only to all parties but also to all Member States and the Community institutions even if they did not intervene in the case before the CFI.[15] That extended provision for notification is plainly designed to enable Member States and Community institutions to make use of their right to bring an appeal even where they did not intervene in the proceedings before the CFI.[16]

The CFI is required to give a decision as to costs in its final judgment or in the order which closes proceedings.[17] The unsuccessful party is ordered to pay the costs if they have been asked for in the successful party's pleading.[18] Where there are several unsuccessful parties, the CFI decides how the costs are to be shared.[19] When each party succeeds on some heads and fails on others, or where the circumstances are exceptional, the CFI may order the parties to bear

---

9 Statute, Article 32.
10 Decision, Article 2(3), fourth sub-paragraph.
11 Statute, Article 34; ECJ Rules of Procedure, Article 64(2).
12 Statute, Articles 33 and 35; ECJ Rules of Procedure, Article 63.
13 Statute, Article 34; ECJ Rules of Procedure, Article 64(1). The judgment is binding from the date of its delivery: ECJ Rules of Procedure, Article 65.
14 ECJ Rules of Procedure, Article 64(2).
15 Statute, Article 48.
16 Pursuant to the third paragraph of Article 49 of the Statute.
17 Statute, Article 35; ECJ Rules of Procedure, Article 69(1).
18 ECJ Rules of Procedure, Article 69(2), first sub-paragraph.
19 ECJ Rules of Procedure, Article 69(2), second sub-paragraph.

their own costs in whole or in part;[20] and it may order even a successful party to pay costs which it considers that party to have unreasonably or vexatiously caused the opposite party to incur.[1] A party who discontinues or withdraws from proceedings is ordered to pay the costs, unless the discontinuance or withdrawal was justified by the conduct of the opposite party;[2] but if the opposite party has not asked for costs, the parties bear their own costs.[3]

A special rule applies to the award of costs in staff cases. In proceedings commenced by an official or other servant against an institution, the institution bears its own costs, even if successful. However, the CFI may order the official or servant to pay costs which it considers him to have unreasonably or vexatiously caused the institution to incur.[4]

Special forms of procedure

In addition to the normal stages of procedure, provision is made for a number of special forms of procedure. They include judgments in default of defence and applications to set them aside,[5] third party proceedings to contest a judgment rendered without that party being heard,[6] proceedings for the revision of a judgment on discovery of a decisive new fact[7] and applications for the interpretation of a judgment.[8] However, the most prominent of the special forms of procedure are the summary procedure, the steps on 'procedural issues' and the intervention procedure.

The CFI has jurisdiction to suspend the application of an act contested in proceedings before it,[9] to prescribe any necessary interim measures in any case before it[10] and to suspend the enforcement of judgments of the CFI or of decisions of the Council or of the Commission which impose a pecuniary obligation on persons other

---

20 ECJ Rules of Procedure, Article 69(3), first sub-paragraph.
 1 ECJ Rules of Procedure, Article 69(3), second sub-paragraph.
 2 ECJ Rules of Procedure, Article 69(4), first sub-paragraph.
 3 ECJ Rules of Procedure, Article 69(4), second sub-paragraph.
 4 ECJ Rules of Procedure, Article 70; see also *idem*, Article 69(3), second sub-paragraph.
 5 Statute, Article 38; ECJ Rules of Procedure, Article 94.
 6 Statute, Article 39; ECJ Rules of Procedure, Article 97.
 7 Statute, Article 41; ECJ Rules of Procedure, Articles 98 to 100.
 8 Statute, Article 40; ECJ Rules of Procedure, Article 102.
 9 ECSC Treaty, Article 39, second paragraph, EEC Treaty, Article 185, and Euratom Treaty, Article 157; applied to the CFI by Article 4 of the Decision.
10 ECSC Treaty, Article 39, third paragraph, EEC Treaty, Article 186, and Euratom Treaty, Article 158; applied to the CFI by Article 4 of the Decision.

than States.[11] Applications for such interlocutory relief fall to be dealt
with by a special summary procedure which is laid down in the Rules of
Procedure.[12]

An application for interlocutory relief must be made by a separate
document.[13] Such an application must comply with the rules as to the
form and content of applications in main actions.[14] In addition it must
state the subject-matter of the dispute, the circumstances giving rise to
urgency and the factual and legal grounds establishing a *prima facie* case
for the interim measures applied for.[15]

An application for interlocutory relief is decided on by the President
of the CFI unless he decides to refer it to the full court.[16] The application
for interlocutory relief is served on the opposite party, and the President
prescribes a short period within which the opposite party may submit
written or oral observations.[17] In the normal course the order is not
made until the opposite party has submitted observations. However,
the President of the CFI may grant the application even before the
observations of the opposite party have been submitted, in which case
he may subsequently vary or cancel the order, even of his own motion.[18]

The decision on the application for interlocutory relief takes the form
of a reasoned order, which is served on the parties forthwith.[19] The
parties may appeal to the ECJ against the decision within two months of
service; and the appeal is also heard by way of the summary procedure.[20]
The enforcement of the order may be made conditional on the lodging
by the applicant of security, of an amount and nature to be fixed in the
light of the circumstances.[1] The practice followed by the President of the

---

11 ECSC Treaty, Articles 44 and 92, third paragraph, EEC Treaty, Articles 187 and
   192, fourth paragraph, and Euratom Treaty, Articles 159 and 164, third paragraph;
   applied to the CFI by Article 4 of the Decision. See also Chapter 3 'The Jurisdiction
   of the CFI' above.
12 Statute, Article 36, first paragraph. The Rules of Procedure concerned will be those
   of the CFI when they are adopted, but until then are those of the ECJ applied to the
   CFI *mutatis mutandis*.
13 ECJ Rules of Procedure, Article 83(3).
14 ECJ Rules of Procedure, Article 83(3), applying *idem* Articles 37 and 38, as to which
   see the text in relation to applications above.
15 ECJ Rules of Procedure, Article 83(2).
16 Statute, Article 36, first paragraph; ECJ Rules of Procedure, Article 85, first paragraph. If the President of the CFI is absent or prevented from attending, his place is
   taken by the most senior of the Presidents of Chamber who is available, failing whom
   his place is taken by the most senior of the judges available: Statute, Article 36,
   second paragraph; ECJ Rules of Procedure, Article 85, second paragraph.
17 ECJ Rules of Procedure, Article 84(1).
18 ECJ Rules of Procedure, Article 84(2).
19 ECJ Rules of Procedure, Article 86(1).
20 Statute, Article 50, second and third paragraphs. Those provisions exclude the
   application of Article 86(1) of the ECJ Rules of Procedure in so far as it does not
   allow an appeal.
 1 ECJ Rules of Procedure, Article 86(2).

CFI in this regard may have significant consequences. It is clear that the requirement of a large amount by way of security may make interim measures less attractive to an applicant. Unless the order fixes the date on which the interim measure is to lapse, it lapses automatically when final judgment is delivered in the case.[2] Orders suspending the enforcement of a decision of the CFI or of a measure adopted by another Community institution must fix a date on which the interim measure is to lapse.[3]

The order has only an interim effect and is without prejudice to the CFI's decision on the substance of the case.[4] On application by a party, the order may at any time be varied or cancelled where there has been a change in circumstances.[5] Rejection of an application for an interim measure does not bar the party who made it from making a further application on the basis of new facts.[6] There is no specific provision as to costs on an application for interlocutory relief. The ECJ's practice has been to reserve the costs to be dealt with in the final judgment in the action, and it is conceivable that the CFI will follow a similar practice.

The rules on 'procedural issues'[7] provide for a party to ask the CFI for a decision on a preliminary objection or on any other procedural issue, ie before going into the substance of the case.[8] Thus, instead of lodging a defence, a defendant may submit a preliminary objection to an application on the grounds that it is inadmissible.

Such an application must be made by a separate document.[9] It must state the grounds of fact of law relied on and the form of order sought, and any supporting documents must be annexed to it.[10] As soon as the application has been lodged, the President of the CFI prescribes a period for the opposite party to submit its observations in writing.[11] A hearing on the preliminary objection may also be held.[12] The CFI may either take a decision on the application or reserve its decision for the final judgment.[13] If the CFI take a decision upholding the application, the action is dismissed. If it takes a decision refusing the application or

2 ECJ Rules of Procedure, Article 86(3).
3 ECJ Rules of Procedure, Article 89.
4 Statute, Article 36, third paragraph; ECJ Rules of Procedure, Article 86(4).
5 ECJ Rules of Procedure, Article 87.
6 ECJ Rules of Procedure, Article 88.
7 ECJ Rules of Procedure, Articles 91 and 92. 'Procedural issues' corresponds to *'incidents de procédure'* in the French version.
8 ECJ Rules of Procedure, Article 91(1), first sub-paragraph. 'A preliminary objection or any other procedural issue' corresponds to *'une exception ou un incident sans engager le débat au fond'* in the French version.
9 ECJ Rules of Procedure, Article 91(1), first sub-paragraph.
10 ECJ Rules of Procedure, Article 91(1), second sub-paragraph.
11 ECJ Rules of Procedure, Article 91(2).
12 ECJ Rules of Procedure, Article 91(3).
13 ECJ Rules of Procedure, Article 91(4), first sub-paragraph. In the French version: *'La Cour . . . statue sur la demande ou la joint au fond'*.

if it reserves its decision for the final judgment, the action continues and the President of the CFI must prescribe new time limits for further steps in the proceedings, eg the lodging of a defence.[14]

Where it is clear that the CFI has no jurisdiction to take cognizance of an application purporting to bring a case before it, it may declare the application inadmissible by reasoned order. Such a decision may be taken even before the application is served on the party against whom it is made.[15] (Where, however, the CFI finds that an action is outside its jurisdiction but within that of the ECJ, it must refer the action to the ECJ).[16]

Moreover, at any stage in a case the CFI may of its own motion raise the question whether there exists an absolute bar to proceeding with the case.[17] An absolute bar is a mandatory ground of inadmissibility. For example the time-limits for bringing proceedings before the ECJ and the CFI are mandatory and cannot be waived by the parties or extended by the court. Thus, even if the parties failed to take the point, the CFI could of its own motion raise the question whether an application before it had been lodged out of time. Where the CFI raises such a question, it gives its decision following the same procedure as on a preliminary objection raised by one of the parties.[18]

It is possible to intervene in cases before the CFI. Member States and Community institutions have an automatic right to intervene, but any other person must establish an interest in the result of the case.[19] A person has an interest in the result of a case where the operative part of the final judgment will affect his position. A mere interest in the success of certain of the arguments put forward is not sufficient.[20]

An intervention is limited to supporting the submissions of one of the parties, ie the form of order sought by one or other of the principal parties.[1] An intervener may not raise a different claim from those

---

14　ECJ Rules of Procedure, Article 91(4), second sub-paragraph.
15　ECJ Rules of Procedure, Article 92(1).
16　Statute, Article 47, second paragraph.
17　ECJ Rules of Procedure, Article 92(2). In the French version: '*La Cour peut à tout moment examiner d'office les fins de non-recevoir d'ordre public*'.
18　ECJ Rules of Procedure, Article 92(2).
19　EEC Statute, Article 37, first and second paragraphs; Euratom Statute, Article 38, first and second paragraphs. In cases under the ECSC Treaty, however, all interveners, including Member States and Community institutions, must establish an interest in the result of the case: ECSC Statute, Article 34, first paragraph.
20　See eg, before the ECJ, Case 111/63 *Lemmerz-Werke v High Authority* [1965] ECR 716 at 717, ECJ; Case 56/64 *Consten v Commission* [1966] ECR 382 at 385; and Joined Cases 116, 124, 143/77 *Amylum v Council and Commission* [1978] ECR 893 at 895.
　1　EEC Statute, Article 37, third paragraph; Euratom Statute, Article 38, third paragraph. ECSC Statute, Article 34, second pragraph, is of similar substance although worded slightly differently. In all three provisions, 'submissions' in the English

made by the party he is supporting. He may, on the other hand, put forward different arguments in support of the claim.[2] Indeed, the intervention procedure would have little purpose if that were not so.

An application to intervene must be made within three months of the publication of the notice of commencement of proceedings in the Official Journal of the European Communities.[3] Such an application must comply with the rules on content and form which apply to applications originating proceedings, and it must also contain the description of the case, the description of the parties, the name and permanent residence of the intervener, the reasons for the intervener's interest in the result of the case where appropriate, submissions supporting or opposing the submissions of a party to the original case,[4] an indication of evidence relied on, supporting documents in an annex and the intervener's address for service in Luxembourg.[5] The application to intervene is served on the parties to the original case, who are given an opportunity to submit their written or oral observations.[6]

The CFI gives its decision on the application to intervene in the form of an order.[7] If the CFI dismisses the application to intervene, the applicant may appeal to the ECJ within two weeks of the notification of the decision dismissing the application; the appeal is dealt with by the ECJ under the summary procedure.[8] If the intervention is allowed, the intervener receives a copy of every document served on the parties but, on application by one of the parties, the CFI may omit secret or confidential documents.[9] Upon being allowed to intervene, the intervener must accept the case as he finds it at the time of his intervention, which is to say that he cannot require earlier procedural stages to be re-opened.[10] The President of the CFI prescribes a period within which the intervener is to supply in writing the grounds in support of his submissions.[11] It is noteworthy that the ECJ's Rules of

version corresponds to '*conclusions*' in the French version, which clearly denotes the form of order sought and not submissions in any wider sense.
2 See eg, before the ECJ, Joined Cases 42, 49/59 *SNUPAT v High Authority* [1961] ECR 53 at 75.
3 ECJ Rules of Procedure, Article 93(1).
4 'Submissions' in this context means the form of order sought; cf '*conclusions*' in the French version of ECJ Rules of Procedure, Article 93(2)(e).
5 ECJ Rules of Procedure, Article 93(2), which also makes interveners subject to the rules governing legal representation of parties before the Court.
6 ECJ Rules of Procedure, Article 93(3).
7 ECJ Rules of Procedure, Article 93(3).
8 Statute, Article 50.
9 ECJ Rules of Procedure, Article 93(4).
10 ECJ Rules of Procedure, Article 93(5), first sub-paragraph.
11 ECJ Rules of Procedure, Article 93(5), second sub-paragraph. In the French version: '. . . *l'intervenant expose par écrit ses moyens à l'appui de ses conclusions*'.

Procedure in their present version do not give the principal parties any right to reply to the arguments thus put forward by an intervener. It may be argued that such a rule is unfair on the principal parties, particularly where the intervention raises new arguments for the first time. Moreover, the ECJ's Rules of Procedure provided for such a right of reply before they were amended in 1979.[12] When the CFI adopts its own Rules of Procedure, it may reconsider the question of the principal parties' right to reply to arguments put forward in an intervention.

Unresolved matters regarding the procedure of the CFI

Applying them *mutatis mutandis*, the ECJ's Rules of Procedure seem capable of providing for most aspects of procedure before the CFI. Whilst they do not make detailed provision for the assignment of cases to Chambers and in particular do not provide for specialisation (as the CFI's Rules of Procedure might do), they make sufficient provision on the matter to enable the CFI to proceed case by case. Likewise, although it may be possible for the CFI to improve on the provisions on preparatory enquiries in the ECJ's Rules of Procedure,[13] those rules contain a sufficiently comprehensive range of provisions on the subject to enable proceedings to take their course before the CFI. On the other hand, it is difficult to see how the ECJ's Rules of Procedure can be applied, even by analogy, so as to determine the cases in which the CFI may sit in plenary session.[14] It is even more difficult to see how the ECJ's Rules of Procedure can be interpreted, even *mutatis mutandis*, in such a way as to provide criteria for selecting the cases in which an Advocate General's Opinion is to be delivered, because the ECJ's Rules of Procedure simply assume the presence of an Advocate General in every case. One conceivable solution is that the CFI should appoint an Advocate General in every case until it adopts its own Rules of Procedure providing for a more selective approach. There remains, nevertheless, the question of the procedures for designating the Advocates General from among the Members of the CFI, as to

12 In its pre-1979 version, Article 93(5), second sub-paragraph, provided: 'The President shall prescribe a period within which the intervener is to state in writing the grounds for his submissions, and a period within which the parties to the original case may answer them' (see OJ 1974 L 350, p 1). Since its amendment in 1979, it provides only: 'The President shall prescribe a period within which the intervener is to state in writing the grounds for his submissions' (see OJ 1979 L 238, p 1).
13 See further the discussion in Chapter 8.
14 Cf Decision, Article 2(4).

which the ECJ's Rules of Procedure are of no assistance as they start from the assumption of permanently appointed Advocates General and judges.[15] These are matters that can be adequately elucidated only by the CFI's Rules of Procedure.

The provisions of the Statute relating to procedure apply definitively to the CFI. They lay down basic aspects of procedure, and the CFI's Rules of Procedure are confined to laying down such further and more detailed provisions as may be necessary.[16] It is not possible for the CFI's Rules of Procedure to depart radically from the basics laid down in the Statute; and if the pattern of the measures so far adopted is maintained, it is to be expected that those Rules of Procedure will remain more or less closely modelled on those of the ECJ. In any event the CFI may not act alone in adopting its Rules of Procedure but must do so in agreement with the ECJ and with the unanimous approval of the Council.[17]

15 Cf Decision, Article 2(3).
16 Statute, Article 46, second paragraph.
17 Treaty, Article 168a(4).

5 Appeals to the ECJ

Appeals from the CFI to the ECJ are governed by Articles 49 to 54 of the Statute as well as by the ECJ's Rules of Procedure, in particular Articles 110 to 123.[1]

Matters subject to appeal

Under the first paragraph of Article 49 of the Statute an appeal may be brought before the ECJ against final decisions of the CFI and decisions of the CFI 'disposing of the substantive issues in part only, or disposing of a procedural issue concerning a plea of lack of competence or inadmissibility'.

Final decisions are all decisions which put an end to a case before the CFI. They may include not only judgments but also orders, for example an order holding that there was no need to give a judgment (*'non-lieu à statuer'*). They might also include an order removing a case from the register following a supposed discontinuance by a party, if there were a dispute as to whether there was a discontinuance or whether it was only conditional.

Secondly, appeal lies against a decision of the CFI which settles a point of substance in a case without disposing of the entire case. One decision of that kind would be a judgment establishing liability to damages without settling the quantum of damages.[2] Another such decision would be a judgment such as that of the ECJ in the *Woodpulp Case* by which it ruled separately on the issue of territorial jurisdiction before going on to consider the other issues in the case.[3]

Third, appeal lies against decisions of the CFI on a preliminary point as to whether a case is inadmissible or as to whether the CFI has jurisdiction to deal with a case. Although Article 49 literally speaks of

1 As to the Rules of Procedure, see further Chapter 6 below.
2 Eg Case 74/74 *CNTA v Commission* [1975] ECR 533, ECJ.
3 Judgment of 27 September 1988 in Joined Cases 89, 104, 114, 116, 117–125, 129/85 *Ahlström v Commission* [1988] 4 CMLR 901, ECJ.

'a plea' of lack of competence or inadmissibility, it is thought that the provision may be interpeted so as to cover such points not only when pleaded by parties but also when raised by the CFI of its own motion.

Under Article 50 of the Statute an appeal lies under specific rules against two further categories of decision. Under the first paragraph of the Article an appeal may be brought aginst dismissal by the CFI of an application to intervene, but only by the person whose application was dismissed. Under the second paragraph of the Article, the parties to the proceedings may appeal against decisions of the CFI concerning interim measures, the suspension of an act contested before the CFI or the suspension of the enforcement of decisions of the Council or the Commission imposing a pecuniary obligation. The appeal in both categories is heard and determined by the President of the ECJ by way of the summary procedure under Article 36 of the Statute.

The foregoing provisions do not allow appeal against purely procedural matters, such as extension of time-limits, preparatory enquiries or decisions on legal aid. Moreover, the second paragraph of Article 51 expressly provides that no appeal shall lie to the ECJ regarding only the amount of costs or the party ordered to pay them.

Persons entitled to appeal

Persons entitled to appeal obviously include parties to the original proceedings who have been unsuccessful in whole or in part. Furthermore, those who intervened in the proceedings before the CFI may also appeal, provided that where the intervener is not a Member State or a Community institution the CFI's decision must 'directly affect' him.[4]

Appeals may also be brought by Member States and Community institutions which did not intervene at first instance.[5] A Member State or institution bringing such an appeal is 'in the same position as Member States or institutions which intervened at first instance',[6] which is to say that, like them, it is confined to supporting the submissions of one of the parties at first instance and may not raise a different claim.[7]

The right of appeal for Member States and Community institutions which did not intervene at first instance may be regarded as justified in the interest of the law. On the other hand it may seem excessive to give

4 Statute, Article 49, second paragraph.
5 Statute, Article 49, third paragraph. This does not apply to staff cases.
6 Statute, Article 49, third paragraph, second sentence.
7 Statute, Article 37, third paragraph.

Member States and institutions a second opportunity to intervene in a case where they have already declined one opportunity to intervene and where their doing so may cause hardship to the parties at first instance. This avenue of appeal may be compared with an Attorney General's reference under English law or with a reference under Article 4 of the Protocol on the Interpretation of the Brussels Convention,[8] whereby the competent authority of a Contracting State may in certain circumstances seek a ruling from the ECJ on a case already decided by the courts of his State. However, neither type of reference is allowed to affect the position of the parties under the decision which is the object of the reference, whereas here the same protection is not guaranteed to the parties at first instance. Here, if the appeal succeeds, the appellant may be ordered to bear its own costs or the costs which the appeal has caused an unsuccessful party to incur.[9] The ECJ may also protect the position of the parties at first instance by leaving the decision in force as regards them even if it upholds the appeal.[10] There is, however, no obligation, and both matters are within the discretion of the ECJ. It is to be hoped that the ECJ will make regular use of its powers of protection in order to avoid hardship on parties drawn into appeals by Member States or institutions which did not appear at first instance.

Time for appeal

The general rule is that an appeal must be lodged within two months of notification of the decision appealed against.[11] The two-month period is the same as that laid down in Article 173 of the EEC Treaty for the bringing of annulment actions.

However, appeals against a decision of the CFI dismissing an application to intervene must be brought within two weeks of the notification of the decision.[12] That very short time-limit is designed to avoid delays in proceedings at first instance.

---

8 The Protocol on the Interpretation by the Court of Justice of the Convention of 27 September 1968 on Jurisdiction and the Enforcement of Judgments in Civil and Commercial Matters (OJ 1978 L 304, p 97).
9 ECJ Rules of Procedure, Article 122.
10 Statute, Article 54, third paragraph.
11 Statute, Article 49, first paragraph. See also Statute, Article 50, second paragraph.
12 Statute, Article 50, first paragraph.

Grounds of appeal

Article 168a(1) of the EEC Treaty provides that appeal lies to the ECJ 'on points of law only'. The first paragraph of Article 51 of the Statute repeats that an appeal to the ECJ 'shall be limited to points of law'. The often difficult distinction between questions of law and questions of fact will have to be worked out in the case-law of the ECJ, and it is evident that there will be substantial scope for interpretation in that matter.

The grounds of appeal are: (1) lack of competence of the CFI, (2) a breach of procedure before the CFI which adversely affects the interests of the appellant and (3) infringement of Community law by the CFI.[13] Those grounds of appeal correspond closely to the first three grounds of annulment laid down in Article 173 of the EEC Treaty. However, the fourth ground of annulment laid down in Article 173, misuse of powers, is not repeated as a ground of appeal against a decision of the CFI. It appears that misuse of powers is regarded in this context as being confined to acts of executive bodies and that if a court (here the CFI) were to misdirect itself, the result could only take the form of an excess of jurisdiction, a breach of procedure or an infringement of law, each of which already constitutes a ground of appeal.

The first ground of appeal, lack of competence of the CFI, leaves to the ECJ the final definition of the extent of the CFI's jurisdiction.

In relation to the second ground of appeal, it is specified that not any breach of procedure before the CFI constitutes a ground of appeal but only such a breach of procedure as 'adversely affects the interests of the appellant'. That rider limits the range of procedural points which may be invoked as grounds of appeal to those which affect the outcome of the case.

Suspensory effect

An appeal has no suspensory effect unless the ECJ so orders by way of interim relief. However, a judgment of the CFI declaring a regulation[14] void does not take effect until the expiry of the two-month period allowed for bringing an appeal or, if an appeal is brought, until the appeal is dismissed.[15] That rule is designed to avoid the uncertainty which could result if regulations were annulled by the CFI with immediate effect then restored by the ECJ on appeal.

13 Statute, Article 51, first paragraph.
14 Or in the context of the ECSC Treaty a general decision: ECSC Statute, Article 53.
15 Statute, Article 53.

The decision of the ECJ on the appeal

If an appeal is well founded, the ECJ must 'quash' the decision of the CFI appealed against.[16] Then it may either refer the case back to the CFI for judgment or give final judgment itself where the state of the proceedings so permits.[17]

That rule gives the ECJ broad discretion to give final judgment in a case which is ready to be disposed of, but to decline to adjudicate on complex questions which it considers should first be resolved by the CFI. It is anticipated that the ECJ will give final judgment itself wherever possible with a view to ensuring economy of procedure, but where the disposal of an appeal leaves major issues of fact or law outstanding the case is more likely to be referred back to the CFI. A case might be referred back to the CFI, for instance, where the ECJ quashed a decision of the CFI holding the action inadmissible or holding that no liability to damages had been incurred. Where a case is referred back to the CFI, it is expressly provided that the CFI is bound by the decision of the ECJ on points of law.[18]

When the ECJ quashes a decision of the CFI upon a successful appeal by a Member State or Community institution which did not intervene at first instance, it may, if it considers necessary, state which of the effects of that decision shall be considered as definitive in respect of the parties to the litigation.[19] That rule is modelled on the second paragraph of Article 174 of the EEC Treaty, which allows the ECJ, when annulling a regulation, to state which of the effects of the regulation shall be considered as definitive. In the present context it allows the ECJ to give to the parties to the original proceedings a measure of protection against appeals by Member States and Community institutions which failed to take part in the proceedings at first instance.[20]

16 Statute, Article 54, first paragraph, first sentence.
17 Statute, Article 54, first paragraph, second sentence.
18 Statute, Article 54, second paragraph.
19 Statute, Article 54, third paragraph.
20 See the discussion under 'Persons Entitled to Appeal' above.

6 Procedure on appeal to the ECJ

The procedure on appeal to the ECJ is governed by the Statute, in particular Article 52, and by the Rules of Procedure of the ECJ, in particular Articles 110 to 123, which were inserted in those Rules as a new Title IV headed 'Appeals against Decisions of the Court of First Instance of the European Communities'.[1] Title IV does not, however, constitute a complete, self-contained text governing appeals: it incorporates by reference a substantial number of the provisions of Title II ('Procedure', Articles 37 to 82) and Title III ('Special Forms of Procedure', Articles 83 to 109), some of them subject to modifications.[2] Moreover, it appears that Title I of the ECJ's Rules of Procedure ('Organisation of the Court', Articles 2 to 36) applies in full to appeals without any express provision to that effect, as it applies to all types of proceedings before the ECJ.[3] Likewise it appears that any provisions of Title III of the Statute ('Procedure') which are applicable regardless of the type of procedure and which have not been specifically excluded, also apply to appeals without any express provision to that effect.[4] The relevant provisions therefore have to be pieced together with some care.

The procedure on appeal is basically modelled on the procedure in direct action before the ECJ (eg an infringement action under Article 169 of the Treaty or an annulment action under Article 173), with the substitution or addition of certain features specific to appeals.[5]

---

1 Amendments to the Rules of Procedure of the ECJ of 7 June 1989 (OJ 1989 L 241, p 1; set out in Appendix III below). The former Articles 110 to 113 of those Rules of Procedure, under the heading 'Miscellaneous Provisions', were re-numbered 124 to 127 respectively.
2 See ECJ Rules of Procedure, Articles 112, 114, 115 and 118.
3 That is indicated in particular by the wording of Article 110 of the ECJ Rules of Procedure, which is expressed to be 'without prejudice to the arrangements laid down in Article 29(2)(b) and (c) and the fourth sub-paragraph of Article 29(3) of these Rules'.
4 Eg Article 17 (representation) and Articles 21 (requests for documents or information).
5 As to the procedure of the ECJ generally, see *Halsbury's Laws of England*, 4th Edn, Vol 51, paragraphs 2.194 to 2.264.

Representation

All parties to an appeal have to be represented. Member States and Community institutions are privileged in that they may be represented by an 'agent' who need not necessarily be legally qualified (although such an agent may be assisted by an adviser or by a lawyer entitled to practise before a court of a Member State). Parties other than Member States and Community institutions must be represented by a lawyer entitled to practise before a court of a Member State. University teachers who have a right of audience under their own national law have the same right before the ECJ.[6] In maintaining this position, the Council declined requests from the trade unions to allow staff to be represented in staff cases by persons who were not legally qualified. The privileges, immunities, rights and obligations of agents, advisers and lawyers in appeals are the same as in other types of proceedings.[7]

Languages

In an appeal the language of the case is the language of the decision of the CFI against which the appeal is brought.[8] The language of the case will thus remain the same throughout the proceedings at first instance and on appeal.

By way of exception, the ECJ may authorise another of the official languages of the Community to be used as the language of the case for all or part of the proceedings, at the request of the parties.[9] Moreover, a Member State is entitled to use its official language when intervening in a case before the ECJ, both in writing and orally.[10]

The other provisions concerning languages contained in Articles 29 to 31 of the ECJ's Rules of Procedure apply to appeals as they do to other types of proceedings before the ECJ.

Written procedure

As in other types of proceeding before the ECJ, the procedure on an appeal consists of a written part and an oral part. The procedure on

6 Statute, Article 17; see also Statute, Article 29, second sentence.
7 ECJ Rules of Procedure, Articles 32 to 36.
8 ECJ Rules of Procedure, Article 110.
9 ECJ Rules of Procedure, Article 29(2)(b) and (c).
10 ECJ Rules of Procedure, Article 29(3), fourth sub-paragraph.

appeal differs, however, in that the ECJ may under certain conditions dispense with the hearing of oral argument from the parties.[11]

An appeal is brought by lodging an application called 'an appeal' either at the Registry of the ECJ or at the Registry of the CFI.[12] If the appeal is lodged at the Registry of the CFI it is transmitted immediately to the Registry of the ECJ. In addition, when an appeal is brought (at either Registry), the Registry of the CFI immediately transmits to the Registry of the ECJ the papers in the case at first instance.[13]

An appeal must contain the name and address of the appellant, the names of the other parties at first instance, the grounds on which the appeal is based, the arguments of law relied on and the form of order sought by the appellant.[14] The appeal must be dated, signed by the appellant's agent or lawyer, accompanied by any supporting documents in an annex, and lodged at the ECJ together with five copies for the ECJ and a further copy for every other party to the proceedings.[15] The appeal must state an address for service in Luxembourg and the name of a person authorised to accept service.[16] The lawyer acting for the appellant must lodge at the Registry of the ECJ a certificate that he is entitled to practise before a court of a Member State.[17] Finally, the decision of the CFI appealed against must be attached to the appeal, and the appeal must state the date on which that decision was notified to the appellant, in order to establish compliance with the time-limit for appeal laid down in the Statute.[18] In the event of failure to comply with the last three of the above requirements (address for service, practising certificate and decision appealed against), the Registrar of the ECJ sets the appellant a reasonable period to put the appeal in order.[19]

The matters which may be pleaded in an appeal are specified in Article 113 of the ECJ's Rules of Procedure. An appeal must seek, first, the quashing of the decision of the CFI in whole or in part and, secondly, the same form of order, in whole or in part, as that sought at first instance.[20] It seems that both of these points must be sought in an

---

11 Statute, Article 52, cf Statute, Article 18. As to dispensing with the hearing, see further under 'Oral Procedure' below.
12 ECJ Rules of Procedure, Article 111(1).
13 ECJ Rules of Procedure, Article 111(2).
14 ECJ Rules of Procedure, Article 112(1).
15 ECJ Rules of Procedure, Article 37.
16 ECJ Rules of Procedure, Article 38(2).
17 ECJ Rules of Procedure, Article 38(3).
18 ECJ Rules of Procedure, Article 112(2).
19 ECJ Rules of Procedure, Article 112(3), referring to *idem*, Article 38(7).
20 ECJ Rules of Procedure, Article 113(1). 'Form of order' in the English version of that provision corresponds to *'conclusions'* in the French version.

appeal, the second one in particular so that the ECJ is able to give final judgment where the state of the proceedings so permits.[1]

While an appellant may ask the ECJ to uphold either a part or the whole of the form of order sought at first instance, he is expressly precluded from seeking a different form of order.[2] While it may seem self-evident that a party should not be allowed to seek on appeal a form of order different from that which he himself sought at first instance, it must be remembered that appeals may also be brought by interveners at first instance[3] and even by Member States and Community institutions which did not intervene at first instance.[4] An intervener is confined to supporting the submissions of (ie the form of order sought by) one of the parties;[5] and a Member State or Community institution which brings an appeal although it did not intervene at first instance is in the same position.[6] Thus even where an appeal is brought by an intervener or by a Member State or Community institution which failed to intervene at first instance, they are confined to claiming the same form of order (either in whole or in part) as that sought by one of the main parties to the proceedings at first instance and may not seek a different form of order.

The form of order sought is perforce supported by arguments, and the question arises to what extent new arguments may be adduced on an appeal. In that connection Article 113(2) of the ECJ's Rules of Procedure provides: 'The subject-matter of the proceedings before the Court of First Instance may not be changed in the appeal'. That provision is ambiguous. It plainly imposes some limitation on the raising of new points on appeal, but it leaves the extent of that limitation undefined. That is a problem which will fall to be resolved by the case-law of the ECJ.

It might be thought possible to resolve the problem by drawing a distinction between issues and arguments (or in French '*moyens*'[7] and '*arguments*') and holding that, while new arguments may be advanced on appeal relating to issues already canvassed at first instance, entirely new issues may not be raised. That solution however rests on distinguishing in each case between an issue and an argument, a distinction which may seem too elusive, at least to those not versed in the civil law systems of certain Member States. In any event, unless the

1 Pursuant to Article 54 of the Statute.
2 ECJ Rules of Procedure, Article 113(1), second indent.
3 Under the conditions laid down in the second paragraph of Article 49 of the Statute.
4 Under the terms of the third paragraph of Article 49 of the Statute.
5 Statute, Article 37, third paragraph. 'Submissions' in the English version of that provision corresponds to '*conclusions*' in the French version.
6 Statute, Article 49, third paragraph.
7 '*Moyens*' is variously translated as 'issues' and as 'grounds' (cf ECJ Rules of Procedure, Articles 42(2), 112(1)(c) and 115(2)(c)), which in itself illustrates the difficulty of rendering the concept in English terms.

appeals procedure is to be rendered otiose, it must be permissible to raise at least some wholly new issues on appeal. For instance, if the CFI based a decision on a point of law which it had taken of its own motion and which had not been canvassed by the parties at first instance and if an appeal was brought on the ground that that point of law had been wrongly decided, it is submitted that Article 113(2) should be interpreted as allowing the appeal to be brought notwithstanding that it was based on a new issue. The opposite interpretation would result in excluding the appeal and thus preventing the parties from ventilating the issue at all. A narrow interpretation of Article 113(2), confining the arguments available on appeal to those already rehearsed at first instance, would, it is submitted, risk emptying the appeal procedure of its substance.

Article 113(2) does not in fact mention either arguments or issues, nor does it provide any mechanism for distinguishing between one and the other, from which it may be inferred that it does not require such a distinction to be drawn. It merely requires that the 'subject-matter of the proceedings' must not be changed on appeal.[8] Therefore, it is suggested, Article 113(2) lends itself more readily to the intepretation that it allows any new matters of law to be raised on appeal (regardless of whether they may be categorized as issues or as arguments) provided only that they relate to basically the same case. It is thought that such an interpretation would allow sufficient latitude for an effective appeals procedure.

The problem is complicated by the fact that Member States and Community institutions may bring an appeal even though they did not take part in the proceedings at first instance.[9] While it may be felt acceptable to allow a principal party at first instance substantial latitude to develop new points on appeal, it may seem quite unfair to allow a Member State or Community institution which failed to intervene at first instance to draw the parties at first instance into an appeal on a point of law not raised at first instance and to require the ECJ to rule on that point without the benefit of a decision on it from the CFI. There may therefore be a motive to give Article 113(2) a narrow interpretation in order to impose limits on the exorbitant right of appeal which has been granted to Member States and Community institutions which failed to intervene at first instance. Nevertheless, that factor should not be allowed to dictate an interpretation which would unduly handicap other categories of appellants.

It will fall to the ECJ to strike a balance between these competing factors in establishing its case-law on the point.

---

8 'The subject-matter of the proceedings' in the English version of Article 113(2) corresponds to *'l'objet du litige'* in the French version.
9 Statute, Article 49, third paragraph.

The Registry of the ECJ must serve the appeal on all the parties to the proceedings before the CFI.[10] It appears that 'parties' in this context is used in the broad sense, as including interveners as well as the principal parties.

In addition it appears that the Registry of the ECJ must publish in the Official Journal of the European Communities a notice of the date when the appeal was lodged, the name and residence of the parties, the subject-matter of the dispute, the claims made and a summary of the contentions and main arguments adduced in support.[11]

The parties (including the interveners) to the proceedings at first instance may lodge a response to the appeal. They may take up a position for or against the appellant; hence the use of the neutral term 'response' to describe this pleading. The response must be lodged within two months of service of the appeal.[12] In the normal case[13] no provision is made for extension of time.[14] Thus the appellant and the respondent are both under an identical time-limit. However, in the specific types of appeal governed by Article 50 of the Statute (appeals against a decision of the CFI concerning interim measures or dismissing an application to intervene), the summary procedure applies and the opposite party has 'a short period' prescribed by the President of the ECJ in which to submit observations.[15]

A response must contain the name and address of the party lodging it, the date on which notice of the appeal was served on him, the grounds relied on, the arguments of law raised and the form of order sought. It must also contain an address for service in Luxembourg and the name of a person authorised to accept service, and the lawyer acting for the party must lodge a practising certificate at the Registry of the ECJ.[16] It is not expressly provided that Article 37 applies to responses,[17] but it is submitted that Article 37 should be regarded as applying to all written pleadings in an appeal, including responses. On that basis, a response must also be dated, signed by the party's lawyer, accompanied by all supporting documents in an annex and lodged together with five copies for the ECJ and a copy for every other party to the proceedings.

10 ECJ Rules of Procedure, Article 114.
11 ECJ Rules of Procedure, Article 16(6).
12 ECJ Rules of Procedure, Article 115(1).
13 Provision is made for exceptional cases in the second paragraph of Article 42 of the Statute, according to which no right shall be prejudiced in consequence of the expiry of a time-limit if the party concerned proves the existence of unforeseeable circumstances or of force majeure.
14 Cf ECJ Rules of Procedure, Article 40(2), which allows an extension of time for lodging a defence in a direct action.
15 ECJ Rules of Procedure, Article 84(1).
16 ECJ Rules of Procedure, Article 115(2).
17 ECJ Rules of Procedure, Article 115(2); cf ECJ Rules of Procedure, Article 112(1).

The matters which may be pleaded in a response are specified in Article 116 of the ECJ's Rules of Procedure. A response must seek the dismissal of the appeal in whole or in part or the quashing of the decision of the CFI in whole or in part, which is to say that it may contain a cross-appeal. It must also seek the same form of order, in whole or in part, as that sought at first instance.[18] Like an appeal, a response may not seek a different form of order from that sought at first instance, nor may it change the subject-matter of the proceedings before the CFI.[19] That form of words is the same as that which governs appeals,[20] and the foregoing discussion of that point also applies to responses.

As a general rule there is only one round of written pleadings. Any pleadings beyond the appeal and the response must be expressly authorised by the President of the ECJ upon request, except in the event of a cross-appeal where there is an automatic right to submit a reply within two months.[1] The request to submit such further pleadings must be made within seven days of service of the response or the reply, as the case may be. The President's decision depends on whether he considers such further pleadings necessary in order to enable the party concerned to put forward its point of view or to provide a basis for the decision on the appeal. If a reply or a rejoinder is so authorised, the President of the ECJ prescribes the period within which they are to be submitted.[2]

Article 42(2) of the ECJ's Rules of Procedure applies to the procedure on appeal.[3] It prohibits the raising of any 'fresh issue'[4] in the reply or rejoinder unless based on matters of law or fact which came to light in the course of the written procedure. That provision may be compared to the provisions stipulating that 'the subject-matter of the proceedings before the CFI may not be changed' in the appeal or in the response.[5] The latter formula is broader, and that difference suggests that the latter provisions fall to be interpreted, not as having the same purport as Article 42(2), but as allowing more scope for new matters to be raised in the appeal or the response than in a reply or rejoinder.[6]

18 ECJ Rules of Procedure, Article 116(1).
19 ECJ Rules of Procedure, Article 116.
20 Cf ECJ Rules of Procedure, Article 113.
 1 ECJ Rules of Procedure, Article 117(1) and (2).
 2 ECJ Rules of Procedure, Article 117(3).
 3 ECJ Rules of Procedure, Article 118.
 4 In the French version, 'moyens nouveaux'.
 5 ECJ Rules of Procedure, Article 113(2) and Article 116(2).
 6 That view is consistent with the arguments advanced above: see p 65.

Particular procedural matters

Most of the provisions of the ECJ's Rules of Procedure concerning direct actions are made applicable to proceedings on appeal by Article 118 of those Rules of Procedure.[7] There are, however, some significant omissions, as well as modifications to certain of the rules applied.

Articles 45 to 54 on preparatory enquiries are not made applicable to appeals. The ECJ thus has no power under its Rules of Procedure to carry out measures of enquiry or to examine witnesses or experts on an appeal. It may, nevertheless, request information and the production of documents under Article 21 of the Statute.

Articles 91 and 92 on 'procedural issues' are also not made applicable to appeals. Article 91 makes provision for parties to apply by a separate document for a decision on a procedural issue (eg a plea of inadmissibility). Because that Article does not apply to appeals, a party who wishes to raise an objection of that kind in the context of an appeal may not do so by a separate document (which would set time running separately from the main pleadings) but must incorporate the objection in his main pleadings.

Article 92 makes provision for the ECJ to take such points of its own motion. It is replaced in appeals by Article 119 of the ECJ's Rules of Procedure. Under Article 119, where an appeal is manifestly inadmissible or manifestly unfounded, it may be dismissed by reasoned order. That is a wider power than the ECJ has under Article 92, as it extends to appeals which are manifestly unfounded as well as to those which are manifestly inadmissible. Nevertheless, that power does not amount to a machinery for filtering appeals to the ECJ, such as the requirement of leave to appeal in English law. The ECJ must accept all appeals which are lodged before it, but the power in Article 119 at least removes the necessity for full proceedings on appeals which plainly have no hope of success.

Article 93 of the ECJ's Rules of Procedure, concerning intervention, does apply to appeals, but it is subject to the modifications in Article 123.

7 Article 42(2) on the raising of new issues (mentioned in the previous paragraph), Article 43 on the joinder of cases, Article 44 on the preliminary report by the reporting judge (subject to Article 121), Articles 55 to 62 on oral procedure (subject to Article 120; see further below), Articles 63 to 68 on judgments, Articles 69 to 75 on costs (subject to Article 122; see further below), Article 76 on legal aid, Articles 77 to 78 on discontinuance, Article 79 on the service of documents, Articles 80 to 82 on time-limits, Articles 83 to 90 on the summary procedure concerning suspension of operation or enforcement and other interim measures, Article 93 on intervention (subject to Article 123; see further below), Articles 95 and 96 on cases assigned to chambers, Article 97 on third party proceedings, Articles 98 to 100 on the revision of judgments and Article 102 on the interpretation of judgments.

Together, those Articles govern the procedure on applications to intervene in appeal proceedings before the ECJ.

It seems that those who intervened in the proceedings before the CFI are regarded by virtue of that fact as being parties to the appeal proceedings before the ECJ. That follows from Article 49 of the Statute whereby an intervener may bring an appeal and Article 112 of the ECJ's Rules of Procedure in which the appellant is described as a 'party'.[8] On that basis, an intervener at first instance need not make a separate application for leave to intervene in the appeal before the ECJ, and such applications need only be made by those who took no part in the proceedings at first instance.[9]

An application to intervene in appeal proceedings before the ECJ must be made within three months of the date on which the appeal was lodged.[10] The three months do not run from the date of publication of the notice of the proceedings in the Official Journal, as they do in direct actions.[11] That is a stringent rule because, on the one hand, notice of an appeal is not served on those who took no part in the proceedings at first instance[12] and, on the other, it commonly takes several weeks for notice of proceedings to be published in the Official Journal. Thus time may start to run against a potential intervener before he is aware that an appeal has been brought. On the other hand, if the three-month period were extended by the time needed for publication of the notice of the appeal in the Official Journal, interveners might enjoy substantially more time to prepare their pleadings than the principal parties.

The ECJ decides on an application to intervene in appeal proceedings after hearing the Advocate General.[13] It does not, however, give the parties an opportunity to submit their observations as it does in a direct action.[14] That rule ensures greater economy of procedure. Together with the stringent time-limit, it limits the extent to which interventions may prolong the proceedings on appeal. As in direct actions, no provision is made for the parties to an appeal to reply in writing to the observations of an intervener.

---

8 The tenor of Articles 114 and 115 of the ECJ's Rules of Procedure is also consistent with interveners at first instance being regarded as parties to the appeal proceedings before the ECJ, and it was suggested above that those Articles fall to be so interpreted.
9 Unless they are themselves the appellant Member State or Community institution under the third paragraph of Article 49 of the Statute.
10 ECJ Rules of Procedure, Article 123.
11 Cf ECJ Rules of Procedure, Article 93(1).
12 ECJ Rules of Procedure, Article 114.
13 ECJ Rules of Procedure, Article 123.
14 Cf ECJ Rules of Procedure, Article 93(3).

Oral procedure

The oral procedure in appeals differs from that in other types of proceedings before the ECJ in that the ECJ may under certain conditions dispense with the hearing of oral argument from the parties.[15]

The ECJ may dispense with the hearing only after hearing the Advocate General and the parties and provided that one of the parties does not object on the ground that the written procedure did not enable him fully to defend his point of view.[16] That rule represents a compromise between a body of opinion in favour of allowing the ECJ to dispense with the hearing at its entire discretion and another body of opinion placing great importance on the right of parties to submit oral argument. The rule thus formulated may be interpreted as giving a party an absolute right to insist on a hearing so long as he objects on the ground stated, but it may also (and perhaps more readily) be interpreted as giving the ECJ power to decide whether it considers the party's objection well founded. On the latter interpretation, the ultimate decision on whether to hold a hearing would lie with the ECJ. The resolution of that point of interpretation is a matter for the ECJ.

Even if the hearing of oral argument from the parties is dispensed with, the Advocate General always delivers an Opinion in appeals before the ECJ. As in other types of proceedings before the ECJ, the Opinion is delivered orally.[17]

Costs

The procedure subsequent to the delivery of the Advocate General's Opinion in appeals is similar to that in other types of proceedings before the ECJ, except that certain special rules apply to costs.

It is provided that the ECJ decides on costs either where it dismisses the appeal or where it upholds the appeal and gives final judgment

---

15 Statute, Article 52; ECJ Rules of Procedure, Article 120 (see also ECJ Rules of Procedure, Article 121). Although those provisions speak of dispensing with the 'oral procedure', it is clear that only the hearing is meant. The oral procedure properly so called also comprises the Advocate General's Opinion (Statute, Article 18, fourth paragraph, and ECJ Rules of Procedure, Article 59), which may not be dispensed with (ECJ Rules of Procedure, Article 120(2)). The drafting, particularly of ECJ Rules of Procedure, Article 120(2), is infelicitous in this respect.
16 ECJ Rules of Procedure, Article 120(1).
17 ECJ Rules of Procedure, Article 120(2); cf ECJ Rules of Procedure, Article 59(1).

itself pursuant to Article 54 of the Statute, ie wherever the case ends before it.[18]

The normal rules on costs (contained in Articles 69 to 75 of the ECJ's Rules of Procedure) apply to appeals,[19] with the exception of appeals in staff cases.[20] Under those rules the losing party must be ordered to pay the costs if the winning party has claimed them, and the ECJ must decide how the costs are to be shared if there are several losing parties.[1] Where each party succeeds on some heads and fails on others, or where the circumstances are exceptional, the ECJ may order the parties to bear their own costs in whole or in part; and it may order even a winning party to pay costs which it considers that party to have unreasonably or vexatiously caused the opposite party to incur.[2]

Special provision is made in relation to appeals in staff cases. Where the appeal is brought by a Community institution, Article 70 of the ECJ's Rules of Procedure applies, to the effect that the institution bears its own costs in any event. Where the appeal is brought by a member of staff, that rule does not apply, with the effect that if the staff member loses he may be ordered to pay the costs pursuant to Article 69(2) of the ECJ's Rules of Procedure. However, in such a case the ECJ may derogate from that rule and order the parties to bear all or part of their own costs where so required by equity.[3]

In all appeals, whether in staff cases or other categories of case, Article 69(4) of the ECJ's Rules of Procedure applies if the appeal is withdrawn.[4] It provides that if costs have been claimed the party who withdraws must be ordered to pay them, unless the withdrawal is justified by the conduct of the opposite party. If costs have not been claimed the parties bear their own costs.

Finally, when an appeal brought by a Member State or Community institution which did not intervene at first instance is successful, the ECJ may nevertheless order the appellant to pay the losing party's costs of the appeal or order the parties to bear their own costs.[5] That provision allows the ECJ to give some protection to parties drawn into an appeal by a Member State or Community institution which failed to take part in the proceedings at first instance.[6]

---

18 ECJ Rules of Procedure, Article 122, first paragraph, No provision is yet made for the position where the case is referred back to the CFI for judgment, but it may be anticipated that in that event costs will fall to be dealt with by the CFI.
19 By virtue of Article 118 of the ECJ Rules of Procedure.
20 Dealt with in the next paragraph.
1 ECJ Rules of Procedure, Article 69(2).
2 ECJ Rules of Procedure, Article 69(3).
3 ECJ Rules of Procedure, Article 122, second paragraph.
4 ECJ Rules of Procedure, Article 122, third paragraph.
5 ECJ Rules of Procedure, Article 122, fourth paragraph.
6 See further the discussion of the third paragraph of Article 49 of the Statute in Chapter 5 above.

Conclusion

The procedure on appeal is largely similar to the procedure in direct actions before the ECJ. On appeal, however, there is basically only one round of written pleadings and the ECJ may dispense with the hearing of oral argument from the parties. Moreover, there is no opportunity for the parties to submit separate preliminary objections: they must be incorporated in the main pleadings. The time-limits are also stricter in appeals: the time-limit for applications to intervene starts to run sooner and there is normally no possibility of extending the time-limit for lodging a response. Taken as a whole the procedure on appeal may therefore be described as more expeditious than the procedure in direct actions before the ECJ.

7 Aspects of case-law concerning the CFI

Introduction

At the present stage, the development of the CFI's case-law still lies ahead, but certain questions on the subject may be briefly alluded to.

Authority of the CFI

The first question is whether the CFI is allowed to lay down new law by its decisions. At an early stage there was some suggestion that its role might be confined to applying the law established by the ECJ. However, it is submitted that the CFI will be called upon both *de facto* and *de jure* to make law by its decisions. In the nature of things, some cases before the CFI will raise points not covered by the existing case-law of the ECJ. It is submitted that when the CFI fulfils its duty[1] to 'determine' such cases, its decision on those points will necessarily constitute new law. Under the terms of the Decision[2] the CFI 'shall exercise at first instance the jurisdiction conferred on the Court of Justice by the Treaties establishing the Communities and by the acts adopted in implementation thereof'. It is suggested that the effect of that provision is to transfer to the CFI the whole of the ECJ's jurisdiction in the areas specified, including the power to make law by judicial decision, and the fact that such jurisdiction is exercised only at first instance and subject to a right of appeal does not prevent the decisions of the CFI from constituting a source of law until they are reversed or overruled by the ECJ.

1 Under Article 168a(1) of the Treaty.
2 Article 3(1).

Precedent

A common lawyer might ask whether the CFI was bound by the decisions of the ECJ and whether it was bound by its own decisions. Community law does not, however, comprise a doctrine of precedent as it is known in common law systems. The ECJ has never accepted any formal rule that it is bound by its own prior decisions. In theory it is free to depart from them at will. If the CFI takes the same approach to its own case-law, it will not consider itself bound by its own prior decisions. If its practice follows that of the ECJ, though, it will tend to adhere closely to its own earlier decisions, albeit not regarding itself as formally bound by them.

As to whether the CFI is bound by the ECJ's case-law, the position is somewhat different. In the specific situation where a case is referred back to the CFI after a successful appeal to the ECJ, it is expressly provided in the second paragraph of Article 54 of the Statute that the CFI 'shall be bound by the decision of the Court of Justice on points of law'. As to the position in general there is no explicit provision to the effect that the CFI is bound by the ECJ's case-law. However, one of the grounds of appeal specified in Article 51 of the Statute is 'the infringement of Community law by the Court of First Instance', and the case-law of the ECJ is part of Community law. It is thought therefore that where the case-law of the ECJ is relevant to a point at issue before the CFI and is clear and unambiguous, the CFI is bound to follow it at the risk of having its decision set aside by the ECJ. It is suggested that that would be the case even where the ECJ had reached its decision against the views of its Advocate General. On the other hand, where the CFI was faced with unclear or conflicting decisions of the ECJ, it is submitted that it would be free to take its own view. The exact amount of latitude enjoyed by the CFI remains to be worked out in the case-law over the coming years.

Methods of interpretation

The methods of interpretation used by the ECJ have been developed in relation to the particular characteristics of the texts which the ECJ has been called upon to interpret. Setting prime importance on the need to maintain the momentum of European construction, the ECJ has given pride of place to the teleological method of interpretation, which is the interpretation of a provision on the basis of its object and purpose. The teleological method is generally used in conjunction with the schematic method of interpretation, which involves placing the provision concerned in its context and interpreting it in relation to the broader scheme of which it forms a part. Thirdly the ECJ uses the literal method of interpretation along with the two others just mentioned, but although it is normally the starting point for the ECJ's examination of a text it is seldom the decisive criterion. Indeed, the ECJ has on occasion adopted a construction which was contrary to the clear wording of a provision.[3] In addition to these three main methods of interpretation, the ECJ also uses a number of more specific techniques and aids to interpretation.

It is thought that the CFI will take over the methods of interpretation developed by the ECJ, not necessarily because it is legally bound to do so but rather because they are uniquely suited to Community law texts. However, the question may arise as to whether the CFI will be as bold in some of its constructions as the ECJ has been. First, the prospect of its judgments being subject to appeal may exert a restraining influence. Secondly, the categories of case within its jurisdiction at present, involving as they do a high proportion of individual decisions, may offer it less scope for broad interpretation than some of the cases before the ECJ. It is conceivable, therefore, that the CFI may be more cautious in its approach to interpretation than the ECJ has been.

General principles of law

Drawing on the legal traditions common to the laws of the Member States, the ECJ has recognised the existence of a number of general principles of law as part of Community law. General principles of law recognised by the ECJ include those of acquired rights, equality (or non-discrimination), legal certainty, legitimate expectations, proportionality and the right to a fair hearing.

Since they are regarded as superior in rank, such general principles can be used to review the legality of Community legislation. For example, a Commission decision in the coal and steel area may be annulled on the grounds that it is contrary to the applicant's legitimate expectations;[4] and a Commission decision requesting information under the competition rules may be annulled in so far as it infringes the rights of defence of the undertaking to which it is addressed.[5] Both such categories of case now come within the jurisdiction of the CFI at first instance.

General principles of law may also be used to inform the

3 See eg Case 67/79 *Fellinger v Bundesanstalt für Arbeit* [1980] ECR 535, ECJ.
4 See Case 344/85 *Ferriere San Carlo v Commission* [1987] ECR 4435.
5 See Case 374/87 *Orkem v Commission* and Case 27/88 *Solvay v Commission*, both judgments of 18 October 1989.

interpretation of Community legislation. In the case of *Razzouk and Beydoun v Commission*,[6] for example, the applicants were widowers of Commission officials and had been refused a pension on the grounds that the Staff Regulations provided only for widows' and not widowers' pensions. On the basis of the general principle of equal treatment of men and women, the ECJ read into the Staff Regulations an entitlement to widower's pension and consequently annulled the refusal complained of. It is thought that such a case would now fall within the jurisdiction of the CFI, which would be called upon to use general principles of law in a similar way.

The list of general principles is not closed, and can be added to as circumstances arise. Quite recently the ECJ established the existence of a Community principle of legal professional privilege, which it read into the Community competition rules, in the *AM & S* case.[7] Such a case would now come within the jurisdiction of the CFI, and if the issue in the case was whether or not a certain general principle was recognised in Community law, it would fall to the CFI to decide the issue, if necessary by establishing the existence of a new principle of Community law. As suggested at the beginning of this chapter, the CFI would have not only the power but the duty to do so.

6 Joined Cases 75, 117/82 [1984] ECR 1509.
7 Case 155/79 *AM & S Europe Ltd v Commission* [1982] ECR 1575.

8 Prospects for the future

Practical arrangements for the CFI

As the CFI advances in its tasks it is called upon from day to day to settle a variety of practical points regarding its operation and its relations with the ECJ. Among such points was the numbering of cases. A single system of numbering might have been envisaged, in order to avoid cases changing number on appeal from the CFI to the ECJ. However, it was decided that each court would run its own series of numbers and the cases would be distinguished by the prefix 'C-'[1] for the ECJ and 'T-'[2] for the CFI, thus for example Case C-345/89 and Case T-19/89 respectively.

The CFI and the ECJ may consider co-ordinating their respective hearing times and dates in order to make the best use of the common facilities which they share, particularly the interpretation service. The two courts might envisage arrangements designed to avoid overlap between their respective hearings as far as possible.

Consideration will also have to be given to the publication of the judgments of the CFI. Hitherto, all judgments of the ECJ have been reported in the official reports (the ECR), and the question will arise whether the decisions of the CFI should also be published, and if so whether in the ECR or in separate reports. The ECR has already attained substantial dimensions,[3] and the cost of translation into all official languages is considerable.[4] It may become necessary to envisage selecting cases for publication, limiting the number of languages in which certain cases are published or shortening the length of the report. These are sensitive questions, particularly in the context of providing legal information throughout the European Community.

There will doubtless be many other practical points to be settled by the CFI as it progresses in its work. However one major task which

1 Corresponding to *'Cour de justice'* in French.
2 Corresponding to *'Tribunal de première instance'* in French.
3 For example, five bound volumes running to 4,815 pages for 1982 alone.
4 See the Annual Report of the Court of Auditors concerning the Financial Year 1981, paragraphs 10.10 to 10.19 (OJ 1982 C 344, p 1, at pp 95 to 97).

faces it in the immediate future is the adoption of its Rules of Procedure.

The Rules of Procedure of the CFI

The CFI is required to adopt its Rules of Procedure immediately upon its constitution.[5] In that connection, a number of points fall to be resolved. The two which have aroused most interest are the arrangements regarding Advocates General before the CFI and the provisions which the CFI will adopt on preparatory enquiries, which are regarded as crucial to its fact-finding role. Other outstanding matters include the arrangements for cases to be heard by the CFI in plenary session and the allocation of cases to Chambers possibly specialising by subject-matter.

The CFI's Rules of Procedure regarding Chambers and plenary sessions will necessarily have a different structure from those of the ECJ because they start from the opposite presumption: in the CFI the use of Chambers is the basic rule and sittings in plenary session must be provided for as an exception,[6] whereas the position in the ECJ is the converse.[7] As to their substance, however, it is thought likely that the Rules of Procedure of the CFI in this area, like those of the ECJ, will give the court a broad discretion as to the formation in which it sits, having regard to factors such as the difficulty and importance of the case concerned.

Specialisation by Chambers has not hitherto been practised by the ECJ, but the issue arises more acutely for the CFI because of the split in its jurisdiction between two clearly recognisable types of litigation: staff cases on the one hand and 'economic law' cases on the other. The need for specialisation may depend on the flow of work in each category, which can be expected to vary from time to time, and any arrangements adopted would have to be sufficiently flexible to accommodate such variations. It would also be important to allow for a balance between the different types of work for the members of the CFI. Specialisation may therefore entail complicated practical arrangements, and in the provisional arrangements which it has adopted for its first year of operation the CFI gives no sign of wishing to introduce it.[8]

5 EEC Treaty, Article 168a(4); Decision, Article 11, second paragraph.
6 See Decision, Article 2(4).
7 See ECSC Treaty, Article 32, second paragraph; EEC Treaty, Article 165, second paragraph; Euratom Treaty, Article 137, second paragraph.
8 Decision of the CFI of 4 October 1989 regarding the assignment of cases to the Chambers (OJ 1989 C 281, p 13).

As regards the arrangements for Advocates General, the CFI will have to lay down, on the one hand, the criteria for selecting the cases in which an Opinion is to be delivered and, on the other hand, the procedures for designating the Advocates General from among the members of the CFI.[9] The difficulties concerning these arrangements have been described above,[10] and the framing of the relevant rules will present the CFI with some difficult choices.

Finally, much emphasis has been placed on the need for the CFI to adopt sound fact-finding procedures. The improvement of the fact-finding process has been acknowledged as one of the aims of the establishment of the CFI,[11] and considerable importance has been attached to it, in particular by the authorities and the legal professions in Member States.[12] Accordingly, it is important that the CFI should both adopt sound fact-finding procedures in its Rules of Procedure and use them to good effect in the cases before it.

The ECJ's Rules of Procedure already allow for the adoption of a wide range of measures of enquiry. In particular Article 45(2) provides for the personal appearance of the parties, requests for information and production of documents, oral testimony, experts' reports and inspection of the place or thing in question.[13] In its present practice, however, the ECJ seldom uses those procedures other than to request written information or the production of certain documents, which it supplements by oral questions to the parties at the hearing. In order to improve fact-finding, the CFI need not necessarily provide for measures of enquiry radically different from those in the ECJ's Rules of Procedure: much turns on its making full use of the procedures available to it. Nevertheless, certain improvements on the provisions of the ECJ's Rules of Procedure in this area may be envisaged.

Under the ECJ's Rules of Procedure it is for the ECJ and not the parties to decide on the adoption of any measures of enquiry.[14] In particular, parties may apply for witnesses to be heard, but only the ECJ may decide whether witnesses will be summoned.[15] Likewise, the production of documents is entirely at the discretion of the ECJ.[16] It

9 Decision, Article 2(3), third sub-paragraph.
10 See Chapter 2, under 'Advocates General'.
11 See the fourth recital in the preamble to the Decision.
12 See for example the Fifth Report of the House of Lords Select Committee on the European Communities, Session 1987–88, 'A European Court of First Instance', paragraphs 63 to 65 and 93.
13 Moreover, although the examination of witnesses is basically inquisitorial, it is provided in Article 47(4) of the ECJ's Rules of Procedure that, 'subject to the control of the President, questions may be put to witnesses by the representatives of the parties', which provides an opportunity, albeit limited, for the parties' counsel to examine witnesses themselves.
14 See ECJ Rules of Procedure, Article 45(1).
15 See ECJ Rules of Procedure, Article 47(1).
16 Statute, Article 21; ECJ Rules of Procedure, Article 45(2).

might be considered whether the CFI's Rules of Procedure should include some provision enabling parties to insist that witnesses be heard, certain documents be produced or other measures of enquiry be adopted.

Furthermore, it might be considered whether provision should be made in some measure for the automatic disclosure of documents by the parties. Such a provision would reduce the risk of a relevant document not being produced to the CFI or of a defendant withholding an important document until the rejoinder, and thus depriving the applicant of the opportunity to comment on it in writing.[17] The discovery of documents as practised for example in English courts can provide some guidance in this respect, but in view of its specifically national characteristics it is doubted whether it could be taken over bodily into the procedure of the CFI. It would seem more likely that the CFI could draw inspiration from Article 23 of the ECSC Statute,[18] which provides: 'Where proceedings are instituted against a decision of one of the institutions of the Community, that institution shall transmit to the Court all the documents relating to the case before the Court'.[19] Since such a sweeping disclosure requirement already exists in relation to disputes under the ECSC Treaty, it might be possible to envisage the CFI's Rules of Procedure providing for automatic disclosure of at least certain categories of document in a wider range of cases before it.

When the CFI's Rules of Procedure have been adopted, the question may arise as to the form in which they might best be presented. Although formally the CFI and the ECJ are each responsible for adopting their own Rules of Procedure, there may be advantages particularly for the public in their producing a single book of rules such as the 'White Book'. That would seem consistent with the fact that the CFI is not a separate institution but is 'attached to' the ECJ. Publication need not be confined to the Rules of Procedure in the strict sense. It would also be helpful if all rules and internal decisions affecting practice and procedure, whatever their rank, were published in a convenient form, which is not presently the case.[20]

---

17 The CFI might also deal with the latter eventuality by making specific provision to allow the applicant to comment on such a document in writing.
18 Applied to the CFI by ECSC Statute, Article 46.
19 See also, in the context of staff cases, Staff Regulations, Article 26, seventh paragraph, which provides: 'The personal file shall be confidential and may be consulted only in the offices of the administration. It shall, however, be forwarded to the Court of Justice of the European Communities if an action concerning the official is brought before the Court'.
20 For example, Article 30 of the Rules on the Internal Organisation of the ECJ, which governs access to case files, is at present unpublished even though it is relevant to persons outside the ECJ.

The effect on the ECJ

The transfer of pending cases from the ECJ to the CFI as at 31 October 1989 relieved the ECJ of 151 cases, but it left three times as many (471 cases) still pending before the ECJ.[1] The transfer was thus insufficient to remove the ECJ's backlog. For the future, a number of cases that would have been brought before the ECJ will fall to be brought before the CFI. Thus for a time the number of new cases coming before the ECJ will be reduced owing to the presence of the CFI. However, that reduction is likely soon to be absorbed by growth in the number of cases brought before the ECJ. On the one hand, cases within the ECJ's existing jurisdiction are likely to become more numerous, particularly with cases springing from the large amount of new legislation for '1992'. On the other hand, the ECJ's caseload will be increased by new sources of jurisdiction: first appeals from the CFI, then international agreements conferring jurisdiction on the ECJ such as the Rome Convention on the law applicable to contractual obligations[2] and the Community Patent Convention.[3] Thus the existence of the CFI is unlikely to give the ECJ sufficient leisure to catch up on its backlog.[4]

It remains for the ECJ to seize the opportunity offered by the relative respite resulting from the establishment of the CFI to review its working methods and procedure. In that connection, the Single European Act inserted in the founding Treaties not only a power for the Council to establish a court of first instance[5] but also a power for it to amend Title III of the Statute ('Procedure') without going through

---

1 See Table IV.
2 OJ 1980 L 266, p 1 (convention); OJ 1989 L 48, pp 1 and 17 (interpretation protocols).
3 See OJ 1976 L 17, p 1, and 'Texts Established by the Luxembourg Conference on the Community Patent 1985', Council of The European Communities, 1986.
4 See 'A European Court of First Instance' (cited in footnote 12 above), at paragraph 90: 'Given a judiciary of high calibre and flexible procedures, the new court should improve the administration of justice and take a considerable load off the ECJ. But, while welcoming the proposal, [the Committee] recognise that it falls short of providing a long-term solution. That will call for more drastic changes, most of which are still inhibited by the terms of the Treaties in spite of the amendments brought about by the Single European Act'.

See also Professor Francis G Jacobs, 'Proposals for Reform in the Organisation and Procedure of the Court of Justice of the European Communities: with Special Reference to the Proposed Court of First Instance' in 'Du droit international au droit de l'intégration: Liber Amicorum Pierre Pescatore', Nomos 1987, p 287 at p 298: 'It seems clear that substantial reforms are necessary to save the Community judicial process from creeping paralysis and that the Court of First Instance, although desirable in itself, is only a short-term palliative in the context of the long-term future of the Court of Justice.'
5 ECSC Treaty, Article 32d; EEC Treaty, Article 168a; Euratom Treaty, Article 140a.

the full Treaty amendment procedure which would otherwise apply.[6] The procedure for that purpose is the same as that for the establishment of the CFI and for the consequent adjustments to the Statute under Article 168a(1) and (2), namely a unanimous decision of the Council acting at the request of the ECJ and after consulting the Commission and the European Parliament. There is also power for the ECJ to adopt amendments to its Rules of Procedure subject to the unanimous approval of the Council.[7] In addition the ECJ is free to change matters of practice without any such formality. There are therefore powers for quite extensive reforms. A committee of members has been set up to study the ECJ's procedure and propose changes, which might be put to the Council at the same time as the proposal for the CFI's Rules of Procedure.

It is thought that no single change is likely to resolve all the ECJ's difficulties, but one measure that could have sweeping effects would be to increase the number of members of the ECJ. It is thought unlikely that the Council, having just appointed 12 members to the CFI with the express object of relieving the ECJ of part of its workload, would be prepared in the short term to appoint any new members to the ECJ. Nevertheless, a modest increase in the number of members of the ECJ (as little as, say, two judges and one Advocate General) would take the number of judges of the ECJ over the number at which it would be possible for the ECJ to sit in two plenary formations simultaneously: the number of judges at present is 13, two more judges would bring it up to 15, and the quorum for a plenary session is seven.[8] Such a 'quantum jump' could transform the pace at which cases were heard by the full Court.

Another measure that could have a significant impact in reducing the ECJ's backlog is to remove the existing restrictions on the assignment of cases to Chambers. The five-judge Chamber has proved to be a particularly effective formation for judging cases: small enough to be flexible and responsive, but large enough to develop new case-law with authority. Yet the ECJ is at present not allowed to assign to Chambers any cases brought before it by a Member State or by a Community institution.[9] That rule leads to cases being kept before the full Court when they would be suited to smaller formations. For

---

6 ECSC Treaty, Article 45, second paragraph; EEC Treaty, Article 188, second paragraph; Euratom Treaty, Article 160, second paragraph. The text of those provisions is reproduced in Appendix I. On those provisions, see Professor Antonio Tizzano, 'La Cour de justice et l'Acte unique européen' in *Du droit international au droit de l'intégration* (cited in footnote 4 above), p 691 at pp 723–724.

7 ECSC Statute, Article 55 (formerly numbered 44); EEC Treaty, Article 188, third paragraph; Euratom Treaty, Article 160, third paragraph.

8 Statute, Article 15.

9 See ECSC Treaty, Article 32, third paragraph; EEC Treaty, Article 165, third paragraph; Euratom Treaty, Article 137, third paragraph.

instance a simple uncontested infringement action under Article 169 has to be heard in plenary session, whereas a three-judge Chamber may be considered sufficient to deal with the issues involved. Similarly, it is thought inappropriate for a plenary session of the ECJ to be required to deal with the essentially technical questions arising on claims for non-reimbursement of expenditure under the European Agricultural Guidance and Guarantee Fund (EAGGF) when cases of similar technicality, eg in the area of anti-dumping duties, are generally assigned to a five-judge Chamber when brought by natural or legal persons. If there were good reasons supporting the ECJ's request in 1978[10] to be allowed to assign any type of case to Chambers, those reasons are more pressing now. Moreover, it may be thought that the ECJ as an institution and the Community legal order as a whole have now reached a degree of maturity which would justify the Council's showing less reluctance than it did in 1978. It is submitted that at this stage the only criteria governing the assignment of cases to Chambers should be the difficulty or the importance of the case as assessed by the ECJ, and that all other restrictions could now usefully be abolished.

Apart from those two measures of broad effect, it is thought that careful examination of all aspects of the ECJ's practice and procedure could suggest a number of other, perhaps more limited, changes which could cumulatively contribute to resolving the ECJ's difficulties.

The jurisdiction of the CFI

The fact that the transfer of jurisdiction effected by the Decision has been insufficient to relieve the ECJ of its backlog provides an argument for an early extension of the jurisdiction of the CFI. Under the terms of the Decision,[11] the Council is already committed to re-examining the ECJ's proposal to transfer dumping and subsidy cases after two years of operation of the CFI. It is to be hoped that this time it will accept the proposal, particularly if it seems that by then the case-law of the ECJ has substantially settled the law in the area.

In addition, it is submitted, the inadequacy of the transfer resulting from the Decision provides cogent grounds to extend the jurisdiction of the CFI to all the other categories of case covered by Article 168a of the Treaty but not mentioned in the Decision, eg State aid cases, damages actions in general, cases under arbitration clauses and miscellaneous annulment actions by natural or legal persons. Moreover it could be said that such cases would be more appropriately

10 See under 'Historical Background' in Chapter 1 above.
11 Article 3(3).

heard by a first instance court. State aid cases and damages actions frequently involve the examination of complex facts – the very purpose for which the CFI has been established – and disputes under arbitration clauses are typical of the work of first instance courts.[12]

If both dumping cases and the other excluded categories of case were transferred to the CFI, it would usefully discharge the ECJ even though the number of cases involved would be relatively limited. Indeed, Tables III and IV indicate that some three quarters of the cases covered by Article 168a of the Treaty have already been transferred by the Decision and only the missing quarter remains to be transferred.

Attention therefore turns to other possible sources of jurisdiction for the CFI, such as a transfer of any new jurisdiction conferred on the ECJ. In that connection, a declaration[13] is appended to the Single European Act expressly stating that the provisions defining the CFI's jurisdiction[14] do not prejudice any conferral of judicial competence likely to be provided for in the context of agreements concluded between the Member States. Thus it seems that if a new jurisdiction is conferred on the ECJ, either by an agreement between Member States or by a Community measure such as a decision or a regulation, it should be possible to transfer jurisdiction at first instance to the CFI in so far as the cases involved are of a kind coming within the terms of Article 168a of the Treaty. For instance, measures are currently being prepared to introduce a Community trade mark, which should include arrangements for the settlement of disputes.[15] Jurisdiction in that field could be conferred on the ECJ, and it is conceivable that that jurisdiction might be conferred on the CFI subject to a right of appeal to the ECJ on points of law. Other new jurisdictions might in time be conferred on the CFI in a similar way.

On a longer view, it is possible to imagine more far-reaching extensions of the jurisdiction of the CFI, even though they would involve amendment of the founding Treaties. If, for example, the principle of two-tier jurisdiction which has been introduced with the establishment of the CFI were taken to its logical conclusion, first instance jurisdiction in all direct actions should ultimately be transferred to the CFI.[16] That would leave the ECJ with jurisdiction over appeals from the CFI on the one hand and references for

---

12 See further under 'Matters excluded from the jurisdiction of the CFI' in Chapter 3 above.

13 Entitled 'Declaration on the Court of Justice'.

14 Ie ECSC Treaty, Article 32d(1); EEC Treaty, Article 168a(1); Euratom Treaty, Article 140a(1).

15 See OJ 1980 C 351, p 5, and OJ 1984 C 230, p 1.

16 See Y Galmot, 'Le Tribunal de première instance des Communautés européennes', *Revue française de Droit administratif* 1989, p 567 at p 578.

preliminary rulings from national courts on the other, a more homogeneous jurisdiction corresponding to the task of ensuring uniform interpretation of Community law. The CFI for its part would then become the natural forum for all direct Community actions at first instance. Looking still further ahead, some commentators have even contemplated the possibility of the CFI being the first step on the way to a generalised system of first instance courts sitting in each Member State of the European Communities, with the ECJ exercising only an appellate jurisdiction.[17]

Conclusion

Whatever may be the course of future developments, it seems likely that the establishment of the CFI will not be an end in itself but will be the starting point of a series of further changes. It is hoped that they will all serve to enhance and improve the administration of justice in the European Community.

17 See Professor J A Usher's evidence to the House of Lords Select Committee on the European Communities in 'A European Court of First Instance' (cited in footnote 12 above), at pp 50 and 51.

Appendix I

Treaty provisions concerning the CFI introduced by the Single European Act

1. Provisions added to the ECSC Treaty by the Single European Act

Article 32 d*

1. At the request of the Court of Justice and after consulting the Commission and the European Parliament, the Council may, acting unanimously, attach to the Court of Justice a court with jurisdiction to hear and determine at first instance, subject to a right of appeal to the Court of Justice on points of law only and in accordance with the conditions laid down by the Statute, certain classes of action or proceeding brought by natural or legal persons. That court shall not be competent to hear and determine actions brought by Member States or by Community Institutions or questions referred for a preliminary ruling under Article 41.

2. The Council, following the procedure laid down in paragraph 1, shall determine the composition of that court and adopt the necessary adjustments and additional provisions to the Statute of the Court of Justice. Unless the Council decides otherwise, the provisions of this Treaty relating to the Court of Justice, in particular the provisions of the Protocol on the Statute of the Court of Justice, shall apply to that court.

3. The members of that court shall be chosen from persons whose independence is beyond doubt and who possess the ability required for appointment to judicial office; they shall be appointed by common accord of the Governments of the Member States for a term of six years. The membership shall be partially renewed every three years. Retiring members shall be eligible for reappointment.

4. That court shall establish its rules of procedure in agreement with the Court of Justice. Those rules shall require the unanimous approval of the Council.

Article 45

The Statute of the Court is laid down in a Protocol annexed to this Treaty.

The Council may, acting unanimously at the request of the Court of Justice and after consulting the Commission and the European Parliament, amend the provisions of Title III of the Statute.**

---

* Article added by Article 4 of the SEA.
** Second paragraph added by Article 5 of the SEA.

2. Provisions added to the EEC Treaty by the Single European Act

Article 168a*

1. At the request of the Court of Justice and after consulting the Commission and the European Parliament, the Council may, acting unanimously, attach to the Court of Justice a court with jurisdiction to hear and determine at first instance, subject to a right of appeal to the Court of Justice on points of law only and in accordance with the conditions laid down by the Statute, certain classes of action or proceeding brought by natural or legal persons. That court shall not be competent to hear and determine actions brought by Member States or by Community institutions or questions referred for a preliminary ruling under Article 177.

2. The Council, following the procedure laid down in paragraph I, shall determine the composition of that court and adopt the necessary adjustments and additional provisions to the Statute of the Court of Justice. Unless the Council decides otherwise, the provisions of this Treaty relating to the Court of Justice, in particular the provisions of the Protocol on the Statute of the Court of Justice, shall apply to that court.

3. The members of that court shall be chosen from persons whose independence is beyond doubt and who possess the ability required for appointment to judicial office; they shall be appointed by common accord of the Governments of the Member States for a term of six years. The membership shall be partially renewed every three years. Retiring members shall be eligible for reappointment.

4. That court shall establish its rules of procedure in agreement with the Court of Justice. Those rules shall require the unanimous approval of the Council.

Article 188

The Statute of the Court of Justice is laid down in a separate Protocol.

The Council may, acting unanimously at the request of the Court of Justice and after consulting the Commission and the European Parliament, amend the provisions of Title III of the Statute.**

The Court of Justice shall adopt its rules of procedure. These shall require the unanimous approval of the Council.

---

* Article added by Article 11 of the SEA.
** Second paragraph inserted by Article 12 of the SEA.

3. Provisions added to the Euratom Treaty by the Single European Act

Article 140a*

1. At the request of the Court of Justice and after consulting the Commission and the European Parliament, the Council may, acting unanimously, attach to the Court of Justice a court with jurisdiction to hear and determine at first instance, subject to a right of appeal to the Court of Justice on points of law only and in accordance with the conditions laid down by the Statute, certain classes of action or proceeding brought by natural or legal persons. That court shall not be competent to hear and determine actions brought by Member States or by Community institutions or questions referred for a preliminary ruling under Article 150.

2. The Council, following the procedure laid down in paragraph 1, shall determine the composition of that court and adopt the necessary adjustments and additional provisions to the Statute of the Court of Justice. Unless the Council decides otherwise, the provisions of this Treaty relating to the Court of Justice, in particular the provisions of the Protocol on the Statute of the Court of Justice, shall apply to that court.

3. The members of that court shall be chosen from persons whose independence is beyond doubt and who possess the ability required for appointment to judicial office; they shall be appointed by common accord of the Governments of the Member States for a term of six years. The membership shall be partially renewed every three years. Retiring members shall be eligible for reappointment.

4. That court shall establish its rules of procedure in agreement with the Court of Justice. Those rules shall require the unanimous approval of the Council.

Article 160

The Statute of the Court of Justice is laid down in a separate Protocol.

The Council may, acting unanimously at the request of the Court of Justice and after consulting the Commission and the European Parliament, amend the provisions of Title III of the Statute.**

The Court of Justice shall adopt its rules of procedure. These shall require the unanimous approval of the Council.

* Article added by Article 26 of the SEA.
** Second paragraph inserted by Article 27 of the SEA.

Appendix II

Decision establishing the CFI

COUNCIL DECISION

of 24 October 1988

establishing a Court of First Instance of the European Communities

(88/591/ECSC, EEC, EURATOM)*

THE COUNCIL OF THE EUROPEAN COMMUNITIES,

Having regard to the Treaty establishing the European Coal and Steel Community, and in particular Article 32d thereof,

Having regard to the Treaty establishing the European Economic Community, and in particular Article 168a thereof,

Having regard to the Treaty establishing the European Atomic Energy Community, and in particular Article 140a thereof,

Having regard to the Protocol on the Statute of the Court of Justice of the European Coal and Steel Community, signed in Paris on 18 April 1951,

Having regard to the Protocol on the Statute of the Court of Justice of the European Economic Community, signed in Brussels on 17 April 1957,

Having regard to the Protocol on the Statute of the Court of Justice of the European Atomic Energy Community, signed in Brussels on 17 April 1957,

Having regard to the Protocol on Privileges and Immunities of the European Communities, signed in Brussels on 8 April 1965,

Having regard to the request of the Court of Justice,

Having regard to the opinion of the Commission,

Having regard to the opinion of the European Parliament[1],

Whereas Article 32d of the ECSC Treaty, Article 168a of the EEC Treaty and Article 140a of the EAEC Treaty empower the Council to attach to the Court of Justice a Court of First Instance called upon to exercise important judicial functions and whose members are independent beyond doubt and possess the ability required for performing such functions;

Whereas the aforesaid provisions empower the Council to give the Court of First Instance jurisdiction to hear and determine at first instance, subject to a right of appeal

---

* Corrected version, as published in OJ 1989 C 215, p 1, and [1989] 3 CMLR 458.
[1] OJ 1988 C 187, p 227.

to the Court of Justice on points of law only and in accordance with the conditions laid down by the Statutes, certain classes of action or proceeding brought by natural or legal persons;

Whereas, pursuant to the aforesaid provisions, the Council is to determine the composition of that Court and adopt the necessary adjustments and additional provisions to the Statutes of the Court of Justice;

Whereas, in respect of actions requiring close examination of complex facts, the establishment of a second court will improve the judicial protection of individual interests;

Whereas it is necessary, in order to maintain the quality and effectiveness of judicial review in the Community legal order, to enable the Court to concentrate its activities on its fundamental task of ensuring uniform interpretation of Community law;

Whereas it is therefore necessary to make use of the powers granted by Article 32d of the ECSC Treaty, Article 168a of the EEC Treaty and Article 140a of the EAEC Treaty and to transfer to the Court of First Instance jurisdiction to hear and determine at first instance certain classes of action or proceeding which frequently require an examination of complex facts, that is to say actions or proceedings brought by servants of the Communities and also, in so far as the ECSC Treaty is concerned, by undertakings and associations in matters concerning levies, production, prices, restrictive agreements, decisions or practices and concentrations, and so far as the EEC Treaty is concerned, by natural or legal persons in competition matters,

HAS DECIDED AS FOLLOWS:

Article 1

A Court, to be called the Court of First Instance of the European Communities, shall be attached to the Court of Justice of the European Communities. Its seat shall be at the Court of Justice.

Article 2

1. The Court of First Instance shall consist of 12 members.

2. The members shall elect the President of the Court of First Instance from among their number for a term of three years. He may be re-elected.

3. The members of the Court of First Instance may be called upon to perform the task of an Advocate-General.

It shall be the duty of the Advocate-General, acting with complete impartiality and independence, to make, in open court, reasoned submissions on certain cases brought before the Court of First Instance in order to assist the Court of First Instance in the performance of its task.

The criteria for selecting such cases, as well as the procedures for designating the Advocates-General, shall be laid down in the Rules of Procedure of the Court of First Instance.

A member called upon to perform the task of Advocate-General in a case may not take part in the judgment of the case.

4. The Court of First Instance shall sit in chambers of three or five judges. The composition of the chambers and the assignment of cases to them shall be governed by the Rules of Procedure. In certain cases governed by the Rules of Procedure the Court of First Instance may sit in plenary session.

5. Article 21 of the Protocol on Privileges and Immunities of the European Communities and Article 6 of the Treaty establishing a Single Council and a Single Commission of the European Communities shall apply to the members of the Court of First Instance and to its Registrar.

Article 3

1. The Court of First Instance shall exercise at first instance the jurisdiction conferred on the Court of Justice by the Treaties establishing the Communities and by the acts adopted in implementation thereof:

(a) in disputes between the Communities and their servants referred to in Article 179 of the EEC Treaty and in Article 152 of the EAEC Treaty;

(b) in actions brought against the Commission pursuant to the second paragraph of Article 33 and Article 35 of the ECSC Treaty by undertakings or by associations of undertakings referred to in Article 48 of that Treaty, and which concern individual acts relating to the application of Article 50 and Articles 57 to 66 of the said Treaty;

(c) in actions brought against an institution of the Communities by natural or legal persons pursuant to the second paragraph of Article 173 and the third paragraph of Article 175 of the EEC Treaty relating to the implementation of the competition rules applicable to undertakings.

2. Where the same natural or legal person brings an action which the Court of First Instance has jurisdiction to hear by virtue of paragraph 1 of this Article and an action referred to in the first and second paragraphs of Article 40 of the ECSC Treaty, Article 178 of the EEC Treaty, or Article 151 of the EAEC Treaty, for compensation for damage caused by a Community institution through the act or failure to act which is the subject of the first action, the Court of First Instance shall also have jurisdiction to hear and determine the action for compensation for that damage.

3. The Council will, in the light of experience, including the development of jurisprudence, and after two years of operation of the Court of First Instance, re-examine the proposal by the Court of Justice to give the Court of First Instance competence to exercise jurisdiction in actions brought against the Commission pursuant to the second paragraph of Articles 33 and 35 of the ECSC Treaty by undertakings or by associations of undertakings referred to in Article 48 of that Treaty, and which concern acts relating to the application of Article 74 of the said Treaty as well as in actions brought against an institution of the Communities by natural or legal persons pursuant to the second paragraph of Article 173 and the third paragraph of Article 175 of the EEC Treaty and relating to measures to protect trade within the meaning of Article 113 of that Treaty in the case of dumping and subsidies.

Article 4

Save as hereinafter provided, Article 34, 36, 39, 44 and 92 of the ECSC Treaty, Articles 172, 174, 176, 184 to 187 and 192 of the EEC Treaty, and Articles 147, 149, 156 to 159 and 164 of the EAEC Treaty shall apply to the Court of First Instance.

Article 5

The following provisions shall be inserted after Article 43 of the Protocol on the Statute of the Court of Justice of the European Coal and Steel Community:

'TITLE IV:
THE COURT OF FIRST INSTANCE OF THE EUROPEAN COMMUNITIES

Rules concerning the members of the Court of First Instance and its organization

Article 44

Articles 2, 3, 4, 6 to 9, the first paragraph of Article 13, Article 17, the second paragraph of Article 18 and Article 19 of this Statute shall apply to the Court of First Instance and its members. The oath referred to in Article 2 shall be taken before the Court of Justice and the decisions referred to in Articles 3, 4 and 7 shall be adopted by that Court after hearing the Court of First Instance.

Registrar and staff

Article 45

The Court of First Instance shall appoint its Registrar and lay down the rules governing his service. Articles 9 and 14 of this Statute shall apply to the Registrar of the Court of First Instance *mutatis mutandis*.

The President of the Court of Justice and the President of the Court of First Instance shall determine, by common accord, the conditions under which officials and other servants attached to the Court of Justice shall render their services to the Court of First Instance to enable it to function. Certain officials or other servants shall be responsible to the Registrar of the Court of First Instance under the authority of the President of the Court of First Instance.

Procedure before the Court of First Instance

Article 46

The procedure before the Court of First Instance shall be governed by Title III of this Statute, with the exception of Articles 41 and 42.

Such further and more detailed provisions as may be necessary shall be laid down in the Rules of Procedure established in accordance with Article 32d (4) of this Treaty.

Notwithstanding the fourth paragraph of Article 21 of this Statute, the Advocate-General may take his reasoned submissions in writing.

Article 47

Where an application or other procedural document addressed to the Court of First Instance is lodged by mistake with the Registrar of the Court of Justice it shall be transmitted immediately by that Registrar to the Registrar of the Court of First Instance; likewise, where an application or other procedural document addressed to the Court of Justice is lodged by mistake with the Registrar of the Court of First Instance, it shall be transmitted immediately by that Registrar to the Registrar of the Court of Justice.

Where the Court of First Instance finds that it does not have jurisdiction to hear and determine an action in respect of which the Court of Justice has jurisdiction, it shall refer that action to the Court of Justice; likewise, where the Court of Justice finds that an action falls within the jurisdiction of the Court of First Instance, it shall refer that action to the Court of First Instance, whereupon that Court may not decline jurisdiction.

Where the Court of Justice and the Court of First Instance are seised of cases in which the same relief is sought, the same issue of interpretation is raised or the validity of the same act is called in question, the Court of First Instance may, after hearing the parties, stay the proceedings before it until such time as the Court of Justice shall have delivered judgment. Where applications are made for the same act to be declared void, the Court of First Instance may also decline jurisdiction in order that the Court of Justice may rule on such applications. In the cases referred to in this subparagraph, the Court of Justice may also decide to stay the proceedings before it; in that event, the proceedings before the Court of First Instance shall continue.

Article 48

Final decisions of the Court of First Instance, decisions disposing of the substantive issues in part only, or disposing of a procedural issue concerning a plea of lack of competence or inadmissibility, shall be notified by the Registrar of the Court of First Instance to all parties as well as all Member States and the Community institutions even if they did not intervene in the case before the Court of First Instance.

Appeals to the Court of Justice

Article 49

An appeal may be brought before the Court of Justice, within two months of the notification of the decision appealed against, against final decisions of the Court of First Instance and decisions of that Court disposing of the substantive issues in part only, or disposing of a procedural issue concerning a plea of lack of competence or inadmissibility.

Such an appeal may be brought by any party which has been unsuccessful, in whole or in part, in its submissions. However, interveners other than the Member States and the Community institutions may bring such an appeal only where the decision of the Court of First Instance directly affects them.

With the exception of cases relating to disputes between the Community and its servants, an appeal may also be brought by Member States and Community institutions which did not intervene in the proceedings before the Court of First Instance. Such Member States and institutions shall be in the same position as Member States or institutions which intervened at first instance.

Article 50

Any person whose application to intervene has been dismissed by the Court of First Instance may appeal to the Court of Justice within two weeks of the notification of the decision dismissing the application.

The parties to the proceedings may appeal to the Court of Justice against any decision of the Court of First Instance made pursuant to the second or third paragraphs of Article 39 or the third paragraph of Aricle 92 of the Treaty within two months from their notification.

The appeal referred to in the first two paragraphs of this Article shall be heard and determined under the procedure referred to in Article 33 of this Statute.

Article 51

An appeal to the Court of Justice shall be limited to points of law. It shall lie on the grounds of lack of competence of the Court of First Instance, a breach of procedure before it which adversely affects the interests of the appellant as well as the infringement of Community law by the Court of First Instance.

No appeal shall lie regarding only the amount of the costs or the party ordered to pay them.

Procedure before the Court

Article 52

Where an appeal is brought against a decision of the Court of First Instance, the procedure before the Court of Justice shall consist of a written part and an oral part. In accordance with conditions laid down in the Rules of Procedure the Court of Justice, having heard the Advocate-General and the parties, may dispense with the oral procedure.

Suspensory effect

Article 53

Without prejudice to the second and third paragraphs of Article 39 of this Treaty, an appeal shall not have suspensory effect.

By way of derogation from Article 44 of this Treaty, decisions of the Court of First Instance declaring a general decision to be void shall take effect only as from the date of expiry of the period referred to in the first paragraph of Article 49 of this Statute or, if an appeal shall have been brought within that period, as from the date of dismissal of the appeal, without prejudice, however, to the right of a party to apply to the Court of Justice, pursuant to the second and third paragraphs of Article 39 of this Treaty, for the suspension of the effects of the decision which has been declared void or for the prescription of any other interim measure.

The decision of the Court of Justice on the appeal

Article 54

If the appeal is well founded, the Court of Justice shall quash the decision of the Court of First Instance. It may itself give final judgment in the matter, where the state of the proceedings so permits, or refer the case back to the Court of First Instance for judgment.

Where a case is referred back to the Court of First Instance, that Court shall be bound by the decision of the Court of Justice on points of law.

When an appeal brought by a Member State or a Community institution, which did not intervene in the proceedings before the Court of First Instance, is well founded the Court of Justice may, if it considers this necessary, state which of the effects of the decision of the Court of First Instance which has been quashed shall be considered as definitive in respect of the parties to the litigation.'

Article 6

The former Articles 44 and 45 of the Protocol on the Statute of the Court of Justice of the European Coal and Steel Community shall become Articles 55 and 56 respectively.

Article 7

The following provisions shall be inserted after Article 43 of the Protocol on the Statute of the Court of Justice of the European Economic Community:

'TITLE IV:
THE COURT OF FIRST INSTANCE OF THE EUROPEAN COMMUNITIES

Article 44

Articles 2 to 8, and 13 to 16 of this Statute shall apply to the Court of First Instance and its members. The oath referred to in Article 2 shall be taken before the Court of

Justice and the decisions referred to in Articles 3, 4 and 6 shall be adopted by that Court after hearing the Court of First Instance.

Article 45

The Court of First Instance shall appoint its Registrar and lay down the rules governing his service. Articles 9, 10 and 13 of this Statute shall apply to the Registrar of the Court of First Instance *mutatis mutandis*.

The President of the Court of Justice and the President of the Court of First Instance shall determine, by common accord, the conditions under which officials and other servants attached to the Court of Justice shall render their services to the Court of First Instance to enable it to function. Certain officials or other servants shall be responsible to the Registrar of the Court of First Instance under the authority of the President of the Court of First Instance.

Article 46

The procedure before the Court of First Instance shall be governed by Title III of this Statute, with the exception of Article 20.

Such further and more detailed provisions as may be necessary shall be laid down in the Rules of Procedure established in accordance with Article 168a (4) of this Treaty.

Notwithstanding the fourth paragraph of Article 18 of this Statute, the Advocate-General may make his reasoned submissions in writing.

Article 47

Where an application or other procedural document addressed to the Court of First Instance is lodged by mistake with the Registrar of the Court of Justice it shall be transmitted immediately by that Registrar to the Registrar of the Court of First Instance; likewise, where an application or other procedural document addressed to the Court of Justice is lodged by mistake with the Registrar of the Court of First Instance, it shall be transmitted immediately by that Registrar to the Registrar of the Court of Justice.

Where the Court of First Instance finds that it does not have jurisdiction to hear and determine an action in respect of which the Court of Justice has jurisdiction, it shall refer that action to the Court of Justice; likewise, where the Court of Justice finds that an action falls within the jurisdiction of the Court of First Instance, it shall refer that action to the Court of First Instance, whereupon that Court may not decline jurisdiction.

Where the Court of Justice and the Court of First Instance are seised of cases in which the same relief is sought, the same issue of interpretation is raised or the validity of the same act is called in question, the Court of First Instance may, after hearing the parties, stay the proceedings before it until such time as the Court of Justice shall have delivered judgment. Where applications are made for the same act to be declared void, the Court of First Instance may also decline jurisdiction in order that the Court of Justice may rule on such applications. In the cases referred to in this sub-paragraph, the Court of Justice may also decide to stay the proceedings before it; in that event, the proceedings before the Court of First Instance shall continue.

Article 48

Final decisions of the Court of First Instance, decisions disposing of the substantive issues in part only or disposing of a procedural issue concerning a plea of lack of competence or inadmissibility, shall be notified by the Registrar of the Court of First

Instance to all parties as well as all Member States and the Community institutions even if they did not intervene in the case before the Court of First Instance.

Article 49

An appeal may be brought before the Court of Justice, within two months of the notification of the decision appealed against, against final decisions of the Court of First Instance and decisions of that Court disposing of the substantive issues in part only or disposing of a procedural issue concerning a plea of lack of competence or inadmissibility.

Such an appeal may be brought by any party which has been unsuccessful, in whole or in part, in its submissions. However, interveners other than the Member States and the Community institutions may bring such an appeal only where the decision of the Court of First Instance directly affects them.

With the exception of cases relating to disputes between the Community and its servants, an appeal may also be brought by Member States and Community institutions which did not intervene in the proceedings before the Court of First Instance. Such member States and institutions shall be in the same position as Member States or institutions which intervened at first instance.

Article 50

Any person whose application to intervene has been dismissed by the Court of First Instance may appeal to the Court of Justice within two weeks of the notification of the decision dismissing the application.

The parties to the proceedings may appeal to the Court of Justice against any decision of the Court of First Instance made pursuant to Article 185 or 186 or the fourth paragraph of Article 192 of this Treaty within two months from their notification.

The appeal referred to in the first two paragraphs of this Article shall be heard and determined under the procedure referred to in Article 36 of this Statute.

Article 51

An appeal to the Court of Justice shall be limited to points of law. It shall lie on the grounds of lack of competence of the Court of First Instance, a breach of procedure before it which adversely affects the interests of the appellant as well as the infringement of Community law by the Court of First Instance.

No appeal shall lie regarding only the amount of the costs or the party ordered to pay them.

Article 52

Where an appeal is brought against a decision of the Court of First Instance, the procedure before the Court of Justice shall consist of a written part and an oral part. In accordance with conditions laid down in the Rules of Procedure, the Court of Justice, having heard the Advocate-General and the parties, may dispense with the oral procedure.

Article 53

Without prejudice to Articles 185 and 186 of this Treaty, an appeal shall not have suspensory effect.

By way of derogation from Article 187 of this Treaty, decisions of the Court of First Instance declaring a regulation to be void shall take effect only as from the date of expiry of the period referred to in the first paragraph of Article 49 of this Statute or, if an appeal shall have been brought within that period, as from the date of dismissal of the appeal, without prejudice, however, to the right of a party to apply to the Court of Justice, pursuant to Articles 185 and 186 of this Treaty, for the suspension of the effects of the regulation which has been declared void or for the prescription of any other interim measure.

Article 54

If the appeal is well founded, the Court of Justice shall quash the decision of the Court of First Instance. It may itself give final judgment in the matter, where the state of the proceedings so permits, or refer the case back to the Court of First Instance for judgment.

Where a case is referred back to the Court of First Instance, that Court shall be bound by the decision of the Court of Justice on points of law.

When an appeal brought by a Member State or a Community institution, which did not intervene in the proceedings before the Court of First Instance, is well founded the Court of Justice may, if it considers this necessary, state which of the effects of the decision of the Court of First Instance which has been quashed shall be considered as definitive in respect of the parties to the litigation.'

Article 8

The former Articles 44, 45 and 46 of the Protocol on the Statute of the Court of Justice of the European Economic Community shall become Articles 55, 56 and 57 respectively.

Article 9

The following provisions shall be inserted after Article 44 of the Protocol on the Statute of the Court of the Justice of the European Atomic Energy Community:

'TITLE IV:
THE COURT OF FIRST INSTANCE OF THE EUROPEAN COMMUNITIES

Article 45

Articles 2 to 8, and 13 to 16 of this Statute shall apply to the Court of First Instance and its members. The oath referred to in Article 2 shall be taken before the Court of Justice and the decisions referred to in Articles 3, 4 and 6 shall be adopted by that Court after hearing the Court of First Instance.

Article 46

The Court of First Instance shall appoint its Registrar and lay down the rules governing his service. Articles 9, 10 and 13 of this Statute shall apply to the Registrar of the Court of First Instance *mutatis mutandis*.

The President of the Court of Justice and the President of the Court of First Instance shall determine, by common accord, the conditions under which officials and other servants attached to the Court of Justice shall render their services to the Court of First Instance to enable it to function. Certain officials or other servants shall be responsible to the Registrar of the Court of First Instance under the authority of the President of the Court of First Instance.

Article 47

The procedure before the Court of First Instance shall be governed by Title III of this Statute, with the exception of Articles 20 and 21.

Such further and more detailed provisions as may be necessary shall be laid down in the Rules of Procedure established in accordance with Article 140a (4) of this Treaty.

Notwithstanding the fourth paragraph of Article 18, the Advocate-General may make his reasoned submissions in writing.

Article 48

Where an application or other procedural document addressed to the Court of First Instance is lodged by mistake with the Registrar of the Court of Justice it shall be transmitted immediately by that Registrar to the Registar of the Court of First Instance; likewise, where an application or other procedural document addressed to the Court of Justice is lodged by mistake with the Registrar of the Court of First Instance, it shall be transmitted immediately by that Registrar to the Registrar of the Court of Justice.

Where the Court of First Instance finds that it does not have jurisdiction to hear and determine an action in respect of which the Court of Justice has jurisdiction, it shall refer that action to the Court of Justice; likewise, where the Court of Justice finds that an action falls within the jurisdiction of the Court of First Instance, it shall refer that action to the Court of First Instance, whereupon that Court may not decline jurisdiction.

Where the Court of Justice and the Court of First Instance are seised of cases in which the same relief is sought, the same issue of interpretation is raised or the validity of the same act is called in question, the Court of First Instance may, after hearing the parties, stay the proceedings before it until such time as the Court of Justice shall have delivered judgment. Where applications are made for the same act to be declared void, the Court of First Instance may also decline jurisdiction in order that the Court of Justice may rule on such applications. In the cases referred to in this subparagraph, the Court of Justice may also decide to stay the proceedings before it; in that event, the proceedings before the Court of First Instance shall continue.

Article 49

Final decisions of the Court of First Instance, decisions disposing of the substantive issues in part only or disposing of a procedural issue concerning a plea of lack of competence or inadmissibility, shall be notified by the Registrar of the Court of First Instance to all parties as well as all Member States and the Community institutions even if they did not intervene in the case before the Court of First Instance.

Article 50

An appeal may be brought before the Court of Justice, within two months of the notification of the decision appealed against, against final decisions of the Court of First Instance and decisions of that Court disposing of the substantive issues in part only or disposing of a procedural issue concerning a plea of lack of competence or inadmissibility.

Such an appeal may be brought by any party which has been unsuccessful, in whole or in part, in its submissions. However, interveners other than the Member States and the Community institutions may bring such an appeal only where the decision of the Court of First Instance directly affects them.

With the exception of cases relating to disputes between the Community and its servants, an appeal may also be brought by Member States and Community institutions which did not intervene in the proceedings before the Court of First Instance. Such Member States and institutions shall be in the same position as Member States or institutions which intervened at first instance.

Article 51

Any person whose application to intervene has been dismissed by the Court of First Instance may appeal to the Court of Justice within two weeks of the notification of the decision dismissing the application.

The application to the proceedings may appeal to the Court of Justice against any decision of the Court of First Instance made pursuant to Article 157 or 158 or the third paragraph of Article 164 of this Treaty within two months from their notification.

The appeal referred to in the first two paragraphs of this Article shall be heard and determined under the procedure referred to in Article 37 of this Statute.

Article 52

An appeal to the Court of Justice shall be limited to points of law. It shall lie on the grounds of lack of competence of the Court of First Instance, a breach of procedure before it which adversely affects the interests of the appellant as well as the infringement of Community law by the Court of First Instance.

No appeal shall lie regarding only the amount of the costs or the party ordered to pay them.

Article 53

Where an appeal is brought against a decision of the Court of First Instance, the procedure before the Court of Justice shall consist of a written part and an oral part. In accordance with conditions laid down in the Rules of Procedure the Court of Justice, having heard the Advocate-General and the parties, may dispense with the oral procedure.

Article 54

Without prejudice to Articles 157 and 158 of this Treaty, an appeal shall not have suspensory effect.

By way of derogation from Article 159 of this Treaty, decisions of the Court of First Instance declaring a regulation to be void shall take effect only as from the date of expiry of the period referred to in the first paragraph of Article 50 of this Statute or, if an appeal shall have been brought within that period, as from the date of dismissal of the appeal, without prejudice, however, to the right of a party to apply to the Court of Justice, pursuant to Articles 157 and 158 of this Treaty, for the suspension of the effects of the regulation which has been declared void or for the prescription of any other interim measure.

Article 55

If the appeal is well founded, the Court of Justice shall quash the decision of the Court of First Instance. It may itself give final judgment in the matter, where the state of the proceedings so permits, or refer the case back to the Court of First Instance for judgment.

Where a case is referred back to the Court of First Instance, that Court shall be bound by the decision of the Court of Justice on points of law.

When appeal brought by a Member State or a Community institution, which did not intervene in the proceedings before the Court of First Instance is well founded the Court of Justice may, if it considers this necessary, state which of the effects of the decision of the Court of First Instance which has been quashed shall be considered as definitive in respect of the parties to the litigation.'

Article 10

The former Articles 45, 46 and 47 of the Protocol on the Statute of the Court of Justice of the European Atomic Energy Community shall become Articles 56, 57 and 58 respectively.

Article 11

The first President of the Court of First Instance shall be appointed for three years in the same manner as its members. However, the Governments of the Member States may, by common accord, decide that the procedure laid down in Article 2 (2) shall be applied.

The Court of First Instance shall adopt its Rules of Procedure immediately upon its constitution.

Until the entry into force of the Rules of Procedure of the Court of First Instance, the Rules of Procedure of the Court of Justice shall apply *mutatis mutandis*.

Article 12

Immediately after all members of the Court of First Instance have taken oath, the President of the Council shall proceed to choose by lot the members of the Court of First Instance whose terms of office are to expire at the end of the first three years in accordance with Article 32d (3) of the ECSC Treaty, Article 168a (3) of the EEC Treaty, and Article 140a (3) of the EAEC Treaty.

Article 13

This Decision shall enter into force on the day following its publication in the *Official Journal of the European Communities*, with the exception of Article 3, which shall enter into force on the date of the publication in the *Official Journal of the European Communities* of the ruling by the President of the Court of Justice that the Court of First Instance has been constituted in accordance with law.

Article 14

Cases referred to in Article 3 of which the Court of Justice is seised on the date on which that Article enters into force but in which the preliminary report provided for in Article 44 (1) of the Rules of Procedure of the Court of Justice has not yet been presented shall be referred to the Court of First Instance.

Done at Luxembourg, 24 October 1988.

For the Council
The President
Th. PANGALOS

Appendix III

Rules of procedure applicable before the CFI

RULES OF PROCEDURE OF THE COURT OF JUSTICE OF THE EUROPEAN COMMUNITIES*
(applicable to the CFI *mutatis mutandis* until the entry into force of the CFI's Rules of Procedure)†

INTERPRETATION

Article 1

In these rules:

'ECSC Treaty' means the Treaty establishing the European Coal and Steel Community;

'ECSC Statute' means the Protocol on the Statute of the Court of Justice of the European Coal and Steel Community;

'EEC Treaty' means the Treaty establishing the European Economic Community;

'EEC Statute' means the Protocol on the Statute of the Court of Justice of the European Economic Community;

'Euratom Treaty' means the Treaty establishing the European Atomic Energy Community (Euratom);

'Euratom Statute' means the Protocol on the Statute of the Court of Justice of the European Atomic Energy Community;

For the purposes of these rules, 'institutions' means the institutions of the European Communities and the European Investment Bank.

TITLE 1

ORGANIZATION OF THE COURT

Chapter 1

JUDGES AND ADVOCATES-GENERAL

Article 2

The terms of office of a Judge shall begin on the date laid down in the instrument of his appointment. In the absence of any provision regarding the date, the term shall begin on the date of the instrument.

---

* Adopted on 4 December 1974 (OJ 1974 L 350, p 1), as amended on 12 September 1979 (OJ 1979 L 238, p 1), 27 May 1981 (OJ 1981 L 199, p 1) and 8 May 1987 (OJ 1987 L 165, p 1).
† Decision, Article 11.

Article 3

§ 1

Before taking up his duties, a Judge shall at the first public sitting of the Court which he attends after his appointment take the following oath:

'I swear that I will perform my duties impartially and conscientiously; I swear that I will preserve the secrecy of the deliberations of the Court'.

§ 2

Immediately after taking the oath, a Judge shall sign a solemn declaration by which he undertakes that, both during and after his term of office, he will respect the obligations arising therefrom, and in particular the duty to behave with integrity and discetion as regards the acceptance, after he has ceased to hold office, of certain appointments and benefits.

Article 4

When the Court is called upon to decide whether a Judge no longer fulfils the requisite conditions or no longer meets the obligations arising from his office, the President shall invite the Judge concerned to appear in the Deliberation Room and make his observations; the Registrar shall be absent from the hearing.

Article 5

Articles 2, 3 and 4 of these rules shall apply in a corresponding manner to Advocates-General.

Article 6

Judges and Advocates-General shall rank equally in precedence according to their seniority in office.

Where there is equal seniority in office precedence shall be determined by age.

Retiring Judges and Advocates-General who are reappointed shall retain their former precedence.

Chapter 2

PRESIDENCY OF THE COURT AND CONSTITUTION OF THE CHAMBERS

Article 7

§ 1

The Judges shall, immediately after the partial replacement provided for in Article 32b of the ECSC Treaty, Article 167 of the EEC Treaty and Article 139 of the Euratom Treaty, elect one of their number as President of the Court for a term of three years.

§ 2

If the office of the President of the Court falls vacant before the normal date of expiry thereof, the Court shall appoint a successor for the remainder of the term.

§ 3

The elections provided for in this Article shall be by secret ballot, the Judge obtaining an absolute majority being elected. If no Judge obtains an absolute majority, a second ballot shall be held and the Judge obtaining the most votes shall be elected. Where two or more Judges obtain an equal number of votes the oldest of them shall be deemed elected.

Article 8

The President shall direct the judicial business and the administration of the Court; he shall preside at hearings and at deliberations in the Deliberation Room.

Article 9

§ 1

The Court shall set up Chambers in accordance with the provisions of the second paragraph of Article 32 of the ECSC Treaty, the second paragraph of Article 165 of the EEC Treaty and the second paragraph of Article 137 of the Euratom Treaty and shall decide which judges shall be attached to them.

The composition of the Chambers shall be published in the *Official Journal of the European Communities*.

§ 2

As soon as an application originating proceedings has been lodged, the President shall assign the case to one of the Chambers for any preparatory inquiries and shall designate a Judge from that Chamber to act as Rapporteur.

§ 3

The Court shall lay down general principles governing the assignment of cases to Chambers.

§ 4

These rules shall apply in a corresponding manner to proceedings before the Chambers.

In cases assigned to or devolving upon a Chamber the powers of the President of the Court shall be exercised by the President of the Chamber.

Article 10

§ 1

The Court shall appoint for a period of one year the Presidents of the Chambers and the First Advocate-General.

The provisions of Article 7 (2) and (3) shall apply in a corresponding manner.

Appointments made in pursuance of this paragraph shall be published in the *Official Journal of the European Communities*.

§ 2

The First Advocate-General shall assign each case to an Advocate-General as soon as the Judge-Rapporteur has been designated by the President. He shall take the necessary steps if an Advocate-General is absent or prevented from attending.

Article 11

When the President of the Court is absent or prevented from attending or when the office of President is vacant, the functions of President shall be exercised by a President of a Chamber according to the order of precedence laid down in Article 6 of these rules.

If the President of the Court and the Presidents of the Chambers are all prevented from attending at the same time, or their posts are vacant at the same time, the functions of President shall be exercised by one of the other Judges according to the order of precedence laid down in Article 6 of these rules.

Chapter 3

REGISTRY

Section 1 – the Registrar and Assistant Registrars

Article 12

§ 1

The Court shall appoint the Registrar. Two weeks before the date fixed for making the appointment, the President shall inform the Members of the Court of the applications which have been made for the post.

§ 2

An application shall be accompanied by full details of the candidate's age, nationality, university degrees, knowledge of languages, present and past occupations and experience, if any, in judicial and international fields.

§ 3

The appointment shall be made following the procedure laid down in Article 7 (3) of these rules.

§ 4

The Registrar shall be appointed for a term of six years. He may be reappointed.

§ 5

The Registrar shall take the oath in accordance with Article 3 of these rules.

§ 6

The Registrar may be deprived of his office only if he no longer fulfils the requisite conditions or no longer meets the obligations arising from his office; the Court shall reach its decision after having given the Registrar an opportunity of making his observations.

§ 7

If the office of Registrar falls vacant before the normal date of expiry of the term thereof, the Court shall appoint a new Registrar for a term of six years.

Article 13

The Court may, following the procedure laid down in respect of the Registrar, appoint one or more Assistant Registrars to assist the Registrar and to take his place so far as the Instructions to the Registrar referred to in Article 15 of these rules allow.

Article 14

Where the Registrar and the Assistant Registrars are absent or prevented from attending or their posts are vacant at the same time, the President shall designate an official to carry out temporarily the duties of Registrar.

Article 15

Instructions to the Registrar shall be adopted by the Court acting on a proposal from the President.

Article 16

§ 1

There shall be kept in the Registry, under the control of the Registrar, a register initialled by the President, in which all pleadings and supporting documents shall be consecutively entered in the order in which they are lodged.

§ 2

When a document has been registered, the Registrar shall make a note to that effect on the original and, if a party so requests, on any copy submitted for the purpose.

§ 3

Entries in the register and the notes provided for in the preceding paragraph shall constitute official records.

§ 4

Rules for keeping the register shall be prescribed by the Instructions to the Registrar referred to in Article 15 of these rules.

§ 5

Interested persons may consult the register at the Registry and may obtain copies or extracts on payment of a charge on a scale to be fixed by the Court acting on a proposal from the Registrar.

The parties to a case may on payment of the appropriate charge also obtain copies of pleadings and authenticated copies of judgments and orders.

§ 6

Notice shall be given in the *Official Journal of the European Communities* of the date of registration of an application originating proceedings, the names and permanent residences of the parties, the subject-matter of the dispute, the claims made in the application and a summary of the contentions and of the main arguments adduced in support.

§ 7

Where the Council or the Commission is not a party to a case, the Court shall forward to it copies of the application and of the defence, without the annexes thereto, to enable it to assess whether the inapplicability of one of its acts is being invoked under the third paragraph of Article 36 of the ECSC Treaty, Article 184 of the EEC Treaty or Article 156 of the Euratom Treaty.

Article 17

§ 1

The Registrar shall be responsible, under the authority of the President, for the acceptance, transmission and custody of documents and for effecting such service as is provided for by these rules.

§ 2

The Registrar shall assist the Court, the Chambers, the President and the Judges in all their official functions.

Article 18

The Registrar shall have custody of the seals. He shall be responsible for the records and be in charge of the publications of the Court.

Article 19

Subject to Articles 4 and 27 of these rules, the Registrar shall attend the sittings of the Court and of the Chambers.

Section 2 – Other departments

Article 20

§ 1

The officials and other servants of the Court shall be appointed in accordance with the provisions of the Staff Regulations.

§ 2

Before taking up his duties, an official shall take the following oath before the President, in the presence of the Registrar:

'I swear that I will perform loyally, discreetly and conscientiously the duties assigned to me by the Court of Justice of the European Communities'.

Article 21

The organization of the departments of the Court shall be laid down, and may be modified, by the Court on a proposal from the Registrar.

Article 22

The Court shall set up a translating service staffed by experts with adequate legal training and a thorough knowledge of several official languages of the Court.

Article 23

The Registrar shall be responsible, under the authority of the President, for the administration of the Court, its financial management and its accounts; he shall be assisted in this by an administrator.

Chapter 4

ASSISTANT RAPPORTEURS

Article 24

§ 1

Where the Court is of the opinion that the consideration of and preparatory inquiries in cases before it so require, it shall, pursuant to Article 16 of the ECSC Statute and Articles 12 of the EEC and Euratom Statutes, propose the appointment of Assistant Rapporteurs.

§ 2

Assistant Rapporteurs shall in particular assist the President in connection with applications for the adoption of interim measures and assist the Judge Rapporteurs in their work.

§ 3

In the performance of their duties the Assistant Rapporteurs shall be responsible to the President of the Court, the President of a Chamber or a Judge Rapporteur, as the case may be.

§ 4

Before taking up his duties, an Assistant Rapporteur shall take before the Court the oath set out in Article 3 of these rules.

Chapter 5

THE WORKING OF THE COURT

Article 25

§ 1

The dates and times of the sittings of the Court shall be fixed by the President.

§ 2

The dates and times of the sittings of the Chambers shall be fixed by their respective Presidents.

§ 3

The Court and the Chambers may choose to hold one or more particular sittings in a place other than that where the Court has its seat.

Article 26

§ 1

Where, by reason of a Judge being absent or prevented from attending, there is an even number of Judges, the most junior Judge within the meaning of Article 6 of these rules shall abstain from taking part in the deliberations.

§ 2

If after the Court has been convened it is found that the quorum of seven Judges has not been attained, the President shall adjourn the sitting until there is a quorum.

§ 3

If in any Chamber the quorum of three Judges has not been attained, the President of that Chamber shall so inform the President of the Court who shall designate another Judge to complete the Chamber.

Article 27

§ 1

Deliberations of the Court and Chambers shall take place in the Deliberation Room.

§ 2

Only those Judges who were present at the oral proceedings and the Assistant Rapporteur, if any, entrusted with the consideration of the case may take part in the deliberations.

§ 3

Every Judge taking part in the deliberations shall give his view and the reasons for it.

§ 4

Any Judge may require that any question be formulated in the language of his choice and be communicated in writing to the Court or Chamber before being put to the vote.

§ 5

The opinion reached by the majority of the Judges after final discussion shall determine the decision of the Court. Votes shall be cast in reverse order to the order of precedence laid down in Article 6 of these rules.

§ 6

Differences of view on the substance, wording or order of questions, or on the interpretation of the voting shall be settled by decision of the Court or Chamber.

§ 7

Where the deliberations of the Court concern questions of its own administration, the Advocates-General shall take part and have a vote. The Registrar shall be present, unless the Court decides to the contrary.

§ 8

Where the Court sits without the Registrar being present it shall, if necessary, instruct the most junior Judge within the meaning of Article 6 of these rules to draw up minutes. The minutes shall be signed by this Judge and by the President.

Article 28

§ 1

Subject to any special decision of the Court, its vacations shall be as follows:

- from 18 December to 10 January,
- from the Sunday before Easter to the second Sunday after Easter,
- from 15 July to 15 September.

During the vacations, the functions of President shall be exercised at the place where the Court has its seat either by the President himself, keeping in touch with the Registrar, or by a President of a Chamber or by such other Judge as he may invite to take his place.

§ 2

In a case of urgency, the President may convene the Judges and the Advocates-General during the vacations.

§ 3

The Court shall observe the official holidays of the place where it has its seat.

§ 4

The Court may, in proper circumstances, grant leave of absence to any Judge or Advocate-General.

Chapter 6

LANGUAGES

Article 29

§ 1

The languages of a case shall be Danish, Dutch, English, French, German, Greek, Irish, Italian, Portuguese or Spanish.

§ 2

The language of a case shall be chosen by the applicant, except that:

(a) where the application is made against a Member State or a natural or legal person having the nationality of a Member State, the language of the case shall be the official language of that State; where that State has more than one official language, the applicant may choose between them;

(b) at the joint request of the parties the Court may authorize another of the languages mentioned in paragraph 1 of this Article to be used as the language of the case for all or part of the proceedings;

(c) at the request of one of the parties, and after the opposite party and the Advocate-General have been heard, the Court, may, by way of derogation from sub-paragraphs (a) and (b), authorize another of the languages mentioned in paragraph 1 of this Article to be used as the language of the case for all or part of the proceedings; such a request may not be submitted by an institution of the European Communities.

Where Article 103 of these rules applies, the language of the case shall be the language of the national court or tribunal which refers the matter to the Court.

§ 3

The language of the case shall in particular be used not only in parties' written statements and oral addresses to the Court and in supporting documents but also in the minutes and decisions of the Court.

Supporting documents expressed in any other language must be accompanied by a translation into the language of the case.

In the case of long documents translations may be confined to extracts. However, the Court or Chamber may, of its own motion or at the request of a party, at any time call for a complete or fuller translation.

Notwithstanding the foregoing provisions, a Member State shall be entitled to use its official language when intervening in a case before the Court or when taking part in any reference of a kind mentioned in Article 103. This provision shall apply both to written statements and to oral addresses. The Registrar shall cause any such statement or address to be translated into the language of the case.

§ 4

Where a witness or expert states that he is unable adequately to express himself in one of the languages referred to in paragraph 1 of this Article, the Court or Chamber may authorize him to give his evidence in another language. The Registrar shall arrange for translation into the language of the case.

§ 5

The President of the Court and the Presidents of Chambers in conducting oral proceedings, the Judge Rapporteur both in his preliminary report and in his report at the hearing, Judges and Advocates-General in putting questions and Advocates-General in delivering their opinions may use a language referred to in paragraph 1 of this Article other than the language of the case. The Registrar shall arrange for translation into the language of the case.

Article 30

§ 1

The Registrar shall, at the request of any Judge, of the Advocate-General or of a party, arrange for anything said or written in the course of the proceedings before the Court or a Chamber to be translated into the languages he chooses from those referred to in Article 29 (1).

§ 2

Publications of the Court shall be issued in the languages referred to in Article 1 of Council Regulation No 1.

Article 31

Texts of documents drawn up in the language of the case or in any other language authorized pursuant to Article 29 of these rules shall be authentic.

Chapter 7

RIGHTS AND OBLIGATIONS OF AGENTS, ADVISERS AND LAWYERS

Article 32

§ 1

Agents representing a State or an institution, as well as advisers and lawyers, appearing before the Court or before any judicial authority to whom the Court has addressed letters rogatory, shall enjoy immunity in respect of words spoken or written by them concerning the case or the parties.

§ 2

Agents, advisers and lawyers shall enjoy the following further privileges and facilities:

(a) papers and documents relating to the proceedings shall be exempt from both search and seizure; in the event of a dispute the customs officials or police may seal those papers and documents; they shall then be immediately forwarded to the Court for inspection in the presence of the Registrar and of the person concerned;

(b) agents, advisers and laywers shall be entitled to such allocation of foreign currency as may be necessary for the performance of their duties;

(c) agents, advisers and lawyers shall be entitled to travel in the course of duty without hindrance.

Article 33

In order to qualify for the privileges, immunities and facilities specified in Article 32, persons entitled to them shall furnish proof of their status as follows:

(a) agents shall produce an official document issued by the State or institution which they represent; a copy of this document shall be forwarded without delay to the Registrar by the State or institution concerned;

(b) advisers and lawyers shall produce a certificate signed by the Registrar. The validity of this certificate shall be limited to a specified period, which may be extended or curtailed according to the length of the proceedings.

Article 34

The privileges, immunities and facilities specified in Article 32 of these rules are granted exclusively in the interests of the proper conduct of proceedings.

The Court may waive the immunity where it considers that the proper conduct of proceedings will not be hindered thereby.

Article 35

§ 1

Any adviser or lawyer whose conduct towards the Court, a Chamber, a Judge, an Advocate-General or the Registrar is incompatible with the dignity of the Court, or who uses his rights for purposes other than those for which they were granted, may at any time be excluded from the proceedings by an order of the Court or Chamber, after the Advocate-General has been heard; the person concerned shall be given an opportunity to defend himself.

The order shall have immediate effect.

§ 2

Where an adviser or lawyer is excluded from the proceedings, the proceedings shall be suspended for a period fixed by the President in order to allow the party concerned to appoint another adviser or lawyer.

§ 3

Decisions taken under this Article may be rescinded.

Article 36

The provisions of this Chapter shall apply to university teachers who have a right of audience before the Court in accordance with Article 20 of the ECSC Statute and Articles 17 of the EEC and Euratom Statutes.

TITLE 2

PROCEDURE

Chapter 1

WRITTEN PROCEDURE

Article 37

§ 1

The original of every pleading must be signed by the party's agent or lawyer.

The original, accompanied by all annexes referred to therein, shall be lodged together with five copies for the Court and a copy for every other party to the proceedings. Copies shall be certified by the party lodging them.

§ 2

Institutions shall in addition produce, within time limits laid down by the Court, translations of all pleadings into the other languages provided for by Article 1 of Council Regulation No 1. The second subparagraph of paragraph 1 of this Article shall apply in a corresponding manner.

§ 3

All pleadings shall bear a date. In the reckoning of time limits for taking steps in proceedings, the only relevant date shall be that of lodgment at the Registry.

§ 4

To every pleading there shall be annexed a file containing the documents relied on in support of it, together with a schedule listing them.

§ 5

Where in view of the length of a document only extracts from it are annexed to the pleading, the whole document or a full copy of it shall be lodged at the Registry.

Article 38

§ 1

An application of the kind referred to in Article 22 of the ECSC Statute and Articles 19 of the EEC and Euratom Statutes shall state:

(a) the name and permanent residence of the applicant;

(b) the name of the party against whom the application is made;

(c) the subject matter of the dispute and the grounds on which the application is based;

(d) the form of order sought by the applicant;

(e) the nature of any evidence founded upon by him.

§ 2

For the purpose of the proceedings, the application shall state an address for service in the place where the Court has its seat. It shall also give the name of a person who is authorized and has expressed willingness to accept service.

§ 3

The lawyer acting for a party must lodge at the Registry a certificate that he is entitled to practise before a court of a Member State.

§ 4

The application shall be accompanied, where appropriate, by the documents specified in the second paragraph of Article 22 of the ECSC Statute and in the second paragraph of Articles 19 of the EEC and Euratom Statutes.

§ 5

An application made by a legal person governed by private law shall be accompanied by:

(a) the instrument or instruments constituting and regulating that legal person;

(b) proof that the authority granted to the applicant's lawyer has been properly conferred on him by someone authorized for the purpose.

§ 6

An application submitted under Articles 42 and 89 of the ECSC Treaty, Articles 181 and 182 of the EEC Treaty and Articles 153 and 154 of the Euratom Treaty shall be accompanied by a copy of the arbitration clause contained in the contract governed by private or public law entered into by the Communities or on their behalf, or, as the case may be, by a copy of the special agreement concluded between the Member States concerned.

§ 7

If an application does not comply with the requirements set out in paragraphs 2 to 6 of this Article, the Registrar shall prescribe a reasonable period within which the applicant is to comply with them whether by putting the application itself in order or by producing any of the abovementioned documents. If the applicant fails to put the application in order or to produce the required documents within the time prescribed, the Court shall, after hearing the Advocate-General, decide whether to reject the application on the ground of want of form.

Article 39

The application shall be served on the defendant. In a case where Article 38 (7) applies, service shall be effected as soon as the application has been put in order or the Court has declared it admissible notwithstanding the failure to observe the formal requirements set out in that Article.

Article 40

§ 1

Within one month after service on him of the application, the defendant shall lodge a defence, stating:

(a) the name and permanent residence of the defendant;

(b) the points of fact and law relied on;

(c) the form of order sought;

(d) the nature of any evidence founded upon by him.

The provisions of Article 38 (2) to (5) of these rules shall apply in a corresponding manner to the defence.

§ 2

The time limit laid down in paragraph 1 of this Article may be extended by the President on a reasoned application by the defendant.

Article 41

§ 1

The application originating the proceedings and the defence may be supplemented by a reply from the applicant and by a rejoinder from the defendant.

§ 2

The President shall fix the time limits within which these pleadings are to be lodged.

Article 42

§ 1

In reply or rejoinder a party may indicate further evidence. The party must, however, give reasons for the delay in indicating it.

§ 2

No fresh issue may be raised in the course of proceedings unless it is based on matters of law or of fact which come to light in the course of the written procedure.

If in the course of the written procedure one of the parties raises a fresh issue which is so based, the President may, even after the expiry of the normal procedural time limits, acting on a report of the Judge Rapporteur and after hearing the Advocate-General, allow the other party time to answer on that issue.

The decision on the admissibility of the issue shall be reserved for the final judgment.

Article 43

The Court may, at any time, after hearing the parties and the Advocate-General, order that for the purpose of the written or oral procedure or of its final judgment, a number of related cases concerning the same subject matter shall be dealt with jointly. The decision to join the cases may subsequently be rescinded.

Article 44

§ 1

After the rejoinder provided for in Article 41 (1) of these rules has been lodged, the President shall fix a date on which the Judge-Rapporteur is to present his preliminary report to the Court. The report shall contain recommendations as to whether a preparatory inquiry or any other preparatory step should be undertaken and whether the case should be referred to the Chamber to which it has been assigned under Article 9 (2).

The Court shall decide, after hearing the Advocate-General, what action to take upon the recommendations of the Judge-Rapporteur.

The same procedure shall apply:

(a) where no reply or no rejoinder has been lodged within the time limit fixed in accordance with Article 41 (2) of these Rules;

(b) where the party concerned waives his right to lodge a reply or rejoinder.

§ 2

Where the Court orders a preparatory inquiry and does not undertake it itself, it shall assign the inquiry to the Chamber.

Where the Court decides to open the oral procedure without an inquiry, the President shall fix the opening date.

Chapter 2

PREPARATORY INQUIRIES

Section 1 – Measures of inquiry

Article 45

§ 1

The Court, after hearing the Advocate-General, shall prescribe the measures of inquiry that it considers appropriate by means of an order setting out the issues of fact to be determined. The order shall be served on the parties.

§ 2

Without prejudice to Articles 24 and 25 of the ECSC Statute, Articles 21 and 22 of the EEC Statute or Articles 22 and 23 of the Euratom Statute, the following measures of inquiry may be adopted:

(a) the personal appearance of the parties;

(b) a request for information and production of documents;

(c) oral testimony;

(d) experts' reports;

(e) an inspection of the place or thing in question.

§ 3

The measures of inquiry which the Court has ordered may be conducted by the Court itself, or be assigned to the Judge Rapporteur.

The Advocate-General shall take part in the measures of inquiry.

§ 4

Evidence may be submitted in rebuttal and previous evidence may be amplified.

Article 46

§ 1

A Chamber to which a preparatory inquiry has been assigned may exercise the powers vested in the Court by Articles 45 and 47 to 53 of these rules; the powers vested in the President of the Court may be exercised by the President of the Chamber.

§ 2

Articles 56 and 57 of these rules shall apply in a corresponding manner to proceedings before the Chamber.

§ 3

The parties shall be entitled to attend the measures of enquiry.

Section 2 – The summoning and examination of witnesses and experts

Article 47

§ 1

The Court may, either of its own motion or on application by a party, and after hearing the Advocate-General, order that certain facts be proved by witnesses. The order of the Court shall set out the facts to be proved.

The Court may summon a witness of its own motion or on application by a party or at the instance of the Advocate-General.

An application by a party for the examination of a witness shall state about what facts and for what reasons the witness should be examined.

§ 2

The witness shall be summoned by an order of the Court containing the following information:

(a) the surname, forenames, description and address of the witness;

(b) an indication of the facts about which the witness is to be examined;

(c) where appropriate, particulars of the arrangements made by the Court for reimbursement of expenses incurred by the witness, and of the penalties which may be imposed on defaulting witnesses.

The order shall be served on the parties and the witness.

§ 3

The Court may make the summoning of a witness for whose examination a party has applied conditional upon the deposit with the cashier of the Court of a sum sufficient to cover the taxed costs thereof; the Court shall fix the amount of the payment.

The cashier shall advance the funds necessary in connection with the examination of any witness summoned by the Court of its own motion.

§ 4

After the identity of each witness has been established, the President shall inform him that he will be required to vouch the truth of his evidence in the manner laid down in these rules.

The witness shall give his evidence to the Court, the parties having been given notice to attend. After the witness has given his main evidence the President may, at the request of a party or of his own motion, put questions to him.

The other Judges and the Advocate-General may do likewise.

Subject to the control of the President, questions may be put to witnesses by the representatives of the parties.

§ 5

After giving his evidence, the witness shall take the following oath:

'I swear that I have spoken the truth, the whole truth and nothing but the truth.'

The Court may, after hearing the parties, exempt a witness from taking the oath.

§ 6

The Registrar shall draw up minutes in which the evidence of each witness is reproduced. The minutes shall be signed by the witness and by the Registrar. They shall constitute an official record.

Article 48

§ 1

Witnesses who have been duly summoned shall obey the summons and attend for examination.

§ 2

If a witness who has been duly summoned fails to appear before the Court, the Court may impose upon him a pecuniary penalty not exceeding 250 EMA units of account and may order that a further summons be served on the witness at his own expense.

The same penalty may be imposed upon a witness who, without good reason, refuses to give evidence or to take the oath or where appropriate to make a solemn affirmation in lieu thereof.

§ 3

If a witness upon whom a penalty has been imposed proffers a valid excuse to the Court, the penalty may be cancelled.

§ 4

Penalties imposed and other measures ordered under this Article shall be enforced in accordance with Articles 44 and 92 of the ECSC Treaty, Articles 187 and 192 of the EEC Treaty and Articles 159 and 164 of the Euratom Treaty.

Article 49

§ 1

The Court may order that an expert's report be obtained. The order appointing the expert shall define his task and set a time limit within which he is to make his report.

§ 2

The expert shall receive a copy of the order, together with all documents necessary for carrying out his task. He shall be under the supervision of the Judge-Rapporteur, who may be present during his investigation and who shall be kept informed of his progress in carrying out his task.

§ 3

At the request of the expert, the Court may order the examination of witnesses. Their examination shall be carried out in accordance with Article 47 of these rules.

§ 4

The expert may give his opinion only on points which have been expressly referred to him.

§ 5

After the expert has made his report, the Court may order that he be examined, the parties having been given notice to attend.

Subject to the control of the President, questions may be put to the expert by the representatives of the parties.

§ 6

After making his report, the expert shall take the following oath before the Court:

'I swear that I have conscientiously and impartially carried out my task.'

The Court may, after hearing the parties, exempt the expert from taking the oath.

Article 50

§ 1

If one of the parties objects to a witness or to an expert on the ground that he is not a competent or proper person to act as witness or expert or for any other reason, or if a witness or expert refuses to give evidence, to take the oath or to make a solemn affirmation in lieu thereof, the matter shall be decided upon by the Court.

§ 2

An objection to a witness or to an expert shall be raised within two weeks after service of the order summoning the witness or appointing the expert; the statement of objection must set out the grounds of objection and indicate any evidence founded upon.

Article 51

§ 1

Witnesses and experts shall be entitled to reimbursement of their travel and subsistence expenses. The cashier of the Court may make a payment to them towards these expenses in advance.

§ 2

Witnesses shall be entitled to compensation for loss of earnings, and experts to fees for their services.

The cashier of the Court shall pay witnesses and experts their compensation or fees after they have carried out their respective duties or tasks.

Article 52

The Court may, on application by a party or of its own motion, issue letters rogatory for the examination of witnesses or experts, as provided for in the supplementary rules mentioned in Article 111 of these rules.

Article 53

§ 1

The Registrar shall draw up minutes of every hearing. The minutes shall be signed by the President and by the Registrar and shall constitute an official record.

§ 2

The parties may inspect the minutes and any expert's report at the Registry and obtain copies at their own expense.

Section 3 – Closure of the preparatory inquiry

Article 54

Unless the Court prescribes a period within which the parties may lodge written observations, the President shall fix the date for the opening of the oral procedure after the preparatory inquiry has been completed.

Where a period had been prescribed for the lodging of written observations, the President shall fix the date for the opening of the oral procedure after that period has expired.

Chapter 3

ORAL PROCEDURE

Article 55

§ 1

Subject to the priority of decisions provided for in Article 85 of these rules, the Court shall deal with the cases before it in the order in which the preparatory inquiries in them have been completed. Where the preparatory inquiries in several cases are completed simultaneously, the order in which they are to be dealt with shall be determined by the dates of entry in the register of the applications originating them respectively.

The President may in special circumstances order that a case be given priority over others.

§ 2

On a joint application by the parties the President may order that a case in which the preparatory inquiry has been completed be deferred. In the absence of agreement between the parties the President shall refer the matter to the Court for a decision.

Article 56

§ 1

The proceedings shall be opened and directed by the President, who shall be responsible for the proper conduct of the hearing.

§ 2

The oral proceedings in cases which are heard *in camera* shall not be published.

Article 57

The President may in the course of the hearing put questions to the agents, advisers or lawyers of the parties.

The other Judges and the Advocate-General may do likewise.

Article 58

A party may address the Court only through his agent, adviser or lawyer.

Article 59

§ 1

The Advocate-General shall deliver his opinion orally at the end of the oral procedure.

§ 2

After the Advocate-General has delivered his opinion, the President shall declare the oral procedure closed.

Article 60

The Court may at any time, after hearing the Advocate-General, order any measure of inquiry to be taken or that a previous inquiry be repeated or expanded. The Court may direct the Chamber or the Judge Rapporteur to carry out the measures so ordered.

Article 61

The Court may after hearing the Advocate-General order the reopening of the oral procedure.

Article 62

§ 1

The Registar shall draw up minutes of every hearing. The minutes shall be signed by the President and by the Registrar and shall constitute an official record.

§ 2

The parties may inspect the minutes at the Registry and obtain copies at their own expense.

Chapter 4

JUDGMENTS

Article 63

The judgment shall contain:

- a statement that it is the judgment of the Court,
- the date of its delivery,
- the names of the President and of the Judges taking part in it,
- the name of the Advocate-General,
- the name of the Registrar,
- the description of the parties,
- the names of the agents, advisers and lawyers of the parties,
- the submissions of the parties,
- a statement that the Advocate-General has been heard,
- a summary of the facts,
- the grounds for the decision,
- the operative part of the judgment, including the decision as to costs.

Article 64

§ 1

The judgment shall be delivered in open court; the parties shall be given notice to attend to hear it.

§ 2

The original of the judgment, signed by the President, by the Judges who took part in the deliberations and by the Registrar, shall be sealed and deposited at the Registry; the parties shall be served with certified copies of the judgment.

§ 3

The Registrar shall record on the original of the judgment the date on which it was delivered.

Article 65

The judgment shall be binding from the date of its delivery.

Article 66

§ 1

Without prejudice to the provisions relating to the interpretation of judgments the Court may, of its own motion or on application by a party made within two weeks after the delivery of a judgment, rectify clerical mistakes, errors in calculation and obvious slips in it.

§ 2

The parties, whom the Registrar shall duly notify, may lodge written observations within a period prescribed by the President.

§ 3

The Court shall make its decision in the Deliberation Room after hearing the Advocate-General.

§ 4

The original of the rectification order shall be annexed to the original of the rectified judgment. A note of this order shall be made in the margin of the original of the rectified judgment.

Article 67

If the Court should omit to give a decision on a particular point at issue or on costs, any party may within a month after service of the judgment apply to the Court to supplement its judgment.

The application shall be served on the opposite party and the President shall prescribe a period within which that party may lodge written observations.

After these observations have been lodged, the Court shall, after hearing the Advocate-General, decide both on the admissibility and on the merits of the application.

Article 68

The Registrar shall arrange for the publication of reports of cases before the Court.

Chapter 5

COSTS

Article 69

§ 1

The Court shall give a decision as to costs in its final judgment or in the order which closes the proceedings.

§ 2

The unsuccessful party shall be ordered to pay the costs if they have been asked for in the successful party's pleading.

Where there are several unsuccessful parties the Court shall decide how the costs are to be shared.

§ 3

Where each party succeeds on some and fails on other heads, or where the circumstances are exceptional, the Court may order that the parties bear their own costs in whole or in part.

The Court may order even a successful party to pay costs which the Court considers that party to have unreasonably or vexatiously caused the opposite party to incur.

§ 4

A party who discontinues or withdraws from proceedings shall be ordered to pay the costs, unless the discontinuance or withdrawal is justified by the conduct of the opposite party.

If the opposite party has not asked for costs, the parties shall bear their own costs.

§ 5

Where a case does not proceed to judgment the costs shall be in the discretion of the Court.

Article 70

Without prejudice to the second subparagraph of Article 69 (3) of these rules, in proceedings under Article 95 (3) of these rules, institutions shall bear their own costs.

Article 71

Costs necessarily incurred by a party in enforcing a judgment or order of the Court shall be refunded by the opposite party on the scale in force in the State where the enforcement takes place.

Article 72

Proceedings before the Court shall be free of charge, except that:

(a) where a party has caused the Court to incur avoidable costs the Court may, after hearing the Advocate-General, order that party to refund them;

(b) where copying or translation work is carried out at the request of a party, the cost shall, in so far as the Registrar considers it excessive, be paid for by that party on the scale of charges referred to in Article 16 (5) of these rules.

Article 73

Without prejudice to the preceding Article, the following shall be regarded as recoverable costs:

(a) sums payable to witnesses and experts under Article 51 of these rules;

(b) expenses necessarily incurred by the parties for the purpose of the proceedings, in particular the travel and subsistence expenses and the remuneration of agents, advisers or lawyers.

Article 74

§ 1

If there is a dispute concerning the costs to be recovered, the Chamber to which the case has been assigned shall, on application by the party concerned and after hearing the opposite party and the Advocate-General, make an order, from which no appeal shall lie.

§ 2

The parties may, for the purposes of enforcement, apply for an authenticated copy of the order.

Article 75

§ 1

Sums due from the cashier of the Court shall be paid in the currency of the country where the Court has its seat.

At the request of the person entitled to any sum, it shall be paid in the currency of the country where the expenses to be refunded were incurred or where the steps in respect of which payment is due were taken.

§ 2

Other debtors shall make payment in the currency of their country of origin.

§ 3

Conversions of currency shall be made at the official rates of exchange ruling on the day of payment in the country where the Court has its seat.

Chapter 6

LEGAL AID

Article 76

§ 1

A party who is wholly or in part unable to meet the costs of the proceedings may at any time apply for legal aid.

The application shall be accompanied by evidence of the applicant's need of assistance, and in particular by a document from the competent authority certifying his lack of means.

§ 2

If the application is made prior to proceedings which the applicant wishes to commence, it shall briefly state the subject of such proceedings.

The application need not be made through a lawyer.

§ 3

The President shall designate a Judge to act as Rapporteur. The Chamber to which the latter belongs shall, after considering the written observations of the opposite party and after hearing the Advocate-General, decide whether legal aid should be granted in full or in part, or whether it should be refused. Where there is manifestly no cause of action, legal aid shall be refused.

The Chamber shall make an order without giving reasons, and no appeal shall lie therefrom.

§ 4

The Chamber may at any time, either of its own motion or on application, withdraw legal aid if the circumstances which led to its being granted alter during the proceedings.

§ 5

Where legal aid is granted, the cashier of the Court shall advance the funds necessary to meet the expenses.

In its decision as to costs the Court may order the payment to the cashier of the Court of the whole or any part of amounts advanced as legal aid.

The Registrar shall take steps to obtain the recovery of these sums from the party ordered to pay them.

Chapter 7

DISCONTINUANCE

Article 77

If, before the Court has given its decision, the parties reach a settlement of their dispute and intimate to the Court the abandonment of their claims, the Court shall order the case to be removed from the register.

This provision shall not apply to proceedings under Articles 33 and 35 of the ECSC Treaty, Articles 173 and 175 of the EEC Treaty or Articles 146 and 148 of the Euratom Treaty.

Article 78

If the applicant informs the Court in writing that he wishes to discontinue the proceedings, the Court shall order the case to be removed from the register.

Chapter 8

SERVICE

Article 79

§ 1

Where these rules require that a document be served on a person, the Registrar shall ensure that service is effected at that person's address for service either by the dispatch of a copy of the document by registered post with a form for acknowledgment of receipt or by personal delivery of the copy against a receipt.

The Registrar shall prepare and certify the copies of documents to be served, save where the parties themselves supply the copies in accordance with Article 37 (1) of these rules.

§ 2

The official record of dispatch together with the acknowledgement or the receipt shall be annexed to the original of the document.

Chapter 9

TIME LIMITS

Article 80

§ 1

In the reckoning of any period of time prescribed by the ECSC, EEC or Euratom Treaties, the Statutes of the Court or these rules for the taking of any procedural step, the day of the event from which the period is to run shall be excluded.

Time shall continue to run during vacations.

§ 2

If the period would otherwise end on a Sunday or on an official holiday it shall be extended until the end of the first following working day.

A list of official holidays drawn up by the Court shall be published in the *Official Journal of the European Communities*.

Article 81

§ 1

The period of time allowed for commencing proceedings against a measure adopted by an institution shall run from the day following the receipt by the person concerned of notification of the measure or, where the measure is published, from the 15th day after publication thereof in the *Official Journal of the European Communities*.

§ 2

The extensions, on account of distance, of prescribed time limits shall be provided for in a decision of the Court which shall be published in the *Official Journal of the European Communities*.

Article 82

Any time limit prescribed pursuant to these rules may be extended by whoever prescribed it.

TITLE 3

SPECIAL FORMS OF PROCEDURE

Chapter 1

SUSPENSION OF OPERATION OR ENFORCEMENT AND OTHER INTERIM MEASURES

Article 83

§ 1

An application to suspend the operation of any measure adopted by an institution, made pursuant to the second paragraph of Article 39 of the ECSC Treaty, Article 185 of the EEC Treaty or Article 157 of the Euratom Treaty, shall be admissible only if the applicant is challenging that measure in proceedings before the Court.

An application for the adoption of any other interim measure referred to in the third paragraph of Article 39 of the ECSC Treaty, Article 186 of the EEC Treaty or Article 158 of the Euratom Treaty shall be admissible only if it is made by a party to a case before the Court and relates to that case.

§ 2

An application of a kind referred to in paragraph 1 of this Article shall state the subject matter of the dispute, the circumstances giving rise to urgency and the factual and legal grounds establishing a *prima facie* case for the interim measures applied for.

§ 3

The application shall be made by a separate document and in accordance with the provisions of Articles 37 and 38 of these rules.

Article 84

§ 1

The application shall be served on the opposite party, and the President shall prescribe a short period within which that party may submit written or oral observations.

§ 2

The President may order a preparatory inquiry.

The President may grant the application even before the observations of the opposite party have been submitted. This decision may be varied or cancelled even without any application being made by any party.

Article 85

The President shall either decide on the application himself or refer it to the Court.

If the President is absent or prevented from attending, Article 11 of these rules shall apply in a corresponding manner.

Where the application is referred to it, the Court shall postpone all other cases, and shall give a decision after hearing the Advocate-General. Article 84 shall apply in a corresponding manner.

Article 86

§ 1

The decision on the application shall take the form of a reasoned order, from which no appeal shall lie. The order shall be served on the parties forthwith.

§ 2

The enforcement of the order may be made conditional on the lodging by the applicant of security, of an amount and nature to be fixed in the light of the circumstances.

§ 3

Unless the order fixes the date on which the interim measure is to lapse, the measure shall lapse when final judgment is delivered.

§ 4

The order shall have only an interim effect, and shall be without prejudice to the decision of the Court on the substance of the case.

Article 87

On application by a party, the order may at any time be varied or cancelled on account of a change in circumstances.

Article 88

Rejection of an application for an interim measure shall not bar the party who made it from making a further application on the basis of new facts.

Article 89

The provisions of this Chapter shall apply in a corresponding manner to applications to suspend the enforcement of a decision of the Court or of any measure adopted by another institution, submitted pursuant to Articles 44 and 92 of the ECSC Treaty, Articles 187 and 192 of the EEC Treaty or Articles 159 and 164 of the Euratom Treaty. The order granting the application shall fix a date on which the interim measure is to lapse.

Article 90

§ 1

An application of a kind referred to in the third and fourth paragraphs of Article 81 of the Euratom Treaty shall contain:

  (a) the names and addresses of the persons or undertakings to be inspected;

  (b) an indication of what is to be inspected and of the purpose of the inspection.

§ 2

The President shall give his decision in the form of an order. Article 86 of these rules shall apply in a corresponding manner.

If the President is absent or prevented from attending, Article 11 of these rules shall apply.

Chapter 2

PROCEDURAL ISSUES

Article 91

§ 1

A party wishing to apply to the Court for a decision on a preliminary objection or on any other procedural issue shall make the application by a separate document.

The application must state the grounds of fact and law relied on and the form of order sought by the applicant; any supporting documents must be annexed to it.

§ 2

As soon as the application has been lodged, the President shall prescribe a period within which the opposite party is to lodge a document containing that party's submissions and the grounds for them.

§ 3

Unless the Court decides otherwise, the remainder of the proceedings shall be oral.

§ 4

The Court shall, after hearing the Advocate-General, decide on the application or reserve its decision for the final judgment.

If the Court refuses the application or reserves its decision, the President shall prescribe new time limits for the further steps in the proceedings.

Article 92

§ 1

Where it is clear that the Court has no jurisdiction to take cognizance of an application lodged with it in pursuance of Article 38 (1), the Court may by reasoned order declare the application inadmissible. Such a decision may be adopted even before the application has been served on the party against whom it is made.

§ 2

The Court may at any time of its own motion consider whether there exists any absolute bar to proceeding with a case, and shall give its decision in accordance with Article 91 (3) and (4) of these rules.

Chapter 3

INTERVENTION

Article 93

§ 1

An application to intervene must be made within three months of the publication of the notice referred to in Article 16 (6) of these rules.

§ 2

The application shall contain:

(a) the description of the case;

(b) the description of the parties;

(c) the name and permanent residence of the intervener;

(d) the reasons for the intervener's interest in the result of the case, having regard to Article 37 of the EEC Statute and Article 38 of the Euratom Statute;

(e) submissions supporting or opposing the submissions of a party to the original case;

(f) an indication of any evidence founded upon and, in an annex, the supporting documents;

(g) the intervener's address for service at the place where the Court has its seat.

The intervener shall be represented in accordance with the first and second paragraphs of Article 20 of the ECSC Statute and with Article 17 of the EEC and Euratom Statutes.

Articles 37 and 38 of these rules shall apply in a corresponding manner.

§ 3

The application shall be served on the parties to the original case. The Court shall give the parties an opportunity to submit their written or oral observations and shall, after hearing the Advocate-General, give its decision in the form of an order.

§ 4

If the Court allows the intervention, the intervener shall receive a copy of every document served on the parties. The Court may, however, on application by one of the parties, omit secret or confidential documents.

§ 5

The intervener must accept the case as he finds it at the time of his intervention.

The President shall prescribe a period within which the intervener is to state in writing the grounds for his submissions.

Chapter 4

JUDGMENTS BY DEFAULT AND APPLICATIONS TO SET THEM ASIDE

Article 94

§ 1

If a defendant on whom an application originating proceedings has been duly served fails to lodge a defence to the application in the proper form within the time prescribed, the applicant may apply for judgment by default.

The application shall be served on the defendant. The President shall fix a date for the opening of the oral procedure.

§ 2

Before giving judgment by default the Court shall, after hearing the Advocate-General, consider whether the originating application is admissible, whether the appropriate formalities have been complied with, and whether the applicant's submissions appear well founded. The Court may order a preparatory inquiry.

§ 3

A judgment by default shall be enforceable. The Court may, however, grant a stay of execution until the Court has given its decision on any application under paragraph 4 to set aside the judgment, or it may make execution subject to the provision of security of an amount and nature to be fixed in the light of the circumstances; this security shall be released if no such application is made or if the application fails.

§ 4

Application may be made to set aside a judgment by default.

The application to set aside the judgment must be made within one month from the date of service of the judgment and must be lodged in the form prescribed by Articles 37 and 38 of these rules.

§ 5

After the application has been served, the President shall prescribe a period within which the other party may submit his written observations.

The procedings shall be conducted in accordance with Articles 44 *et seq.* of these rules.

§ 6

The Court shall decide by way of a judgment which may not be set aside. The original of this judgment shall be annexed to the original of the judgment by default. A note of the judgment on the application to set aside shall be made in the margin of the original of the judgment by default.

Chapter 5

CASES ASSIGNED TO CHAMBERS

Article 95

§ 1

The Court may assign to a Chamber any reference for a preliminary ruling of a kind mentioned in Article 103 of these rules as well as any action instituted by a natural or legal person under Article 33 (2), Article 34 (2), Article 35, Article 36 (2), Article 40 (1) and (2), and Article 42 of the ECSC Treaty, Article 172, Article 173 (2), Article 175 (3), Article 178 and Article 181 of the EEC Treaty, and Article 144, Article 146 (2), Article 148 (3), Article 151 and Article 153 of the Euratom Treaty, in so far as the difficulty or the importance of the case or particular circumstances are not such as to require that the Court decide it in plenary session.

§ 2

The decision so to assign a case shall be taken by the Court at the end of the written procedure upon consideration of the preliminary report presented by the Judge-Rapporteur and after the Advocate-General has been heard.

However, a case may not be so assigned if a Member State or an instutition of the Communities, being a party to the proceedings, has requested that the case be decided in plenary sessions. In this sub-paragraph the expression 'party to the proceedings' means any Member State or any institution which is a party to or an intervener in the proceedings or which has submitted written observations in any reference of a kind mentioned in Article 103 of these rules.

§ 3

Proceedings commenced by an official or other servant of an institution against the institution shall, with the exception of applications for the adoption of interim measures, be tried by a Chamber designated each year by the Court for that purpose. Such allocation shall not preclude the adoption of appropriate measures in cases whose subject-matter is related.

§ 4

A Chamber may at any stage refer to the Court any case assigned to or devolving upon it.

Article 96

§ 1

Where an application for the adoption of interim measures is made to the President in the course of proceedings under Article 95 (3) of these rules but the President is absent or prevented from hearing the application, his place shall be taken by the President of the designated Chamber.

§ 2

Without prejudice to his power of referral under Article 85 of these rules, the President may refer the application to the designated Chamber.

Chapter 6

EXCEPTIONAL REVIEW PROCEDURES

Section 1 – Third party proceedings

Article 97

§ 1

Articles 37 and 38 of these rules shall apply in a corresponding manner to an application originating third party proceedings. In addition such an application shall:

(a) specify the judgment contested;

(b) state how that judgment is prejudicial to the rights of the third party;

(c) indicate the reasons why the third party was unable to take part in the original case.

The application must be made against all the parties to the original case.

Where the judgment has been published in the *Official Journal of the European Communities*, the application must be lodged within two months of the publication.

§ 2

The Court may, on application by the third party, order a stay of execution of the judgment. The provisions of Title 3, Chapter 1, of these rules shall apply in a corresponding manner.

§ 3

The contested judgment shall be varied on the points on which the submissions of the third party are upheld.

The original of the judgment in the third party proceedings shall be annexed to the original of the contested judgment. A note of the judgment in the third party proceedings shall be made in the margin of the original of the contested judgment.

Section 2 – Revision

Article 98

An application for revision of a judgment shall be made within three months of the date on which the applicant receives knowledge of the facts on which the application is based.

Article 99

§ 1

Articles 37 and 38 of these rules shall apply in a corresponding manner to an application for revision. In addition such an application shall:

(a) specify the judgment contested;

(b) indicate the points on which the judgment is contested;

(c) set out the facts on which the application is based;

(d) indicate the nature of the evidence to show that there are facts justifying revision of the judgment, and that the time limit laid down in Article 98 has been observed.

§ 2

The application must be made against all parties to the case in which the contested judgment was given.

Article 100

§ 1

Without prejudice to its decision on the merits, the Court sitting in the Deliberation Room shall, after hearing the Advocate-General and having regard to the written observations of the parties, give in the form of a judgment its decision on the admissibility of the application.

§ 2

If the Court finds the application admissible, it shall proceed to consider the merits of the application and shall give its decision in the form of a judgment in accordance with these rules.

§ 3

The original of the revising judgment shall be annexed to the original of the judgment revised. A note of the revising judgment shall be made in the margin of the original of the judgment revised.

Chapter 7

APPEALS AGAINST DECISIONS OF THE ARBITRATION COMMITTEE

Article 101

§ 1

An application originating an appeal under the second paragraph of Article 18 of the Euratom Treaty shall state:

(a) the name and permanent address of the applicant;

(b) the description of the signatory;

(c) a reference to the arbitration committee's decision against which the appeal is made;

(d) the description of the parties;

(e) a summary of the facts;

(f) the grounds of the application and the form of order sought by the applicant.

§ 2

Articles 37 (3) and (4) and 38 (2), (3) and (5) of these rules shall apply in a corresponding manner.

A certified copy of the contested decision shall be annexed to the application.

§ 3

As soon as the application has been lodged, the Registrar of the Court shall request the arbitration committee registry to transmit to the Court the papers in the case.

§ 4

Articles 39, 40, 55 *et seq.* of these rules shall apply in a corresponding manner to these proceedings.

§ 5

The Court shall give its decision in the form of a judgment. Where the Court sets aside the decision of the arbitration committee it may remit the case to the committee.

Chapter 8

INTERPRETATION OF JUDGMENTS

Article 102

§ 1

An application for interpretation of a judgment shall be made in accordance with Articles 37 and 38 of these rules. In addition it shall specify:

(a) the judgment in question;

(b) the passages of which interpretation is sought.

The application must be made against all the parties to the case in which the judgment was given.

§ 2

The Court shall give its decision in the form of a judgment after having given the parties an opportunity to submit their observations and after hearing the Advocate-General.

The original of the interpreting judgment shall be annexed to the original of the judgment interpreted. A note of the interpreting judgment shall be made in the margin of the original of the judgment interpreted.

Chapter 9

PRELIMINARY RULINGS AND OTHER REFERENCES FOR INTEPRETATION

Article 103

§ 1

In cases governed by Article 20 of the EEC Statute and Article 21 of the Euratom Statute, the provisions of Article 43 *et seq.* of these rules shall apply after the statements of case or written observations provided for in the said Articles 20 and 21 have been lodged.

The same provisions shall apply even where such documents are not lodged within the time prescribed in those Articles 20 and 21, or where the parties to the main action, the Member States, the Commission or, as the case may be, the Council declare an intention to dispense with them.

§ 2

The provisions of paragraph 1 shall apply to the references for a preliminary ruling provided for in the Protocol concerning the interpretation by the Court of Justice of the Convention of 29 February 1968 on the Mutual Recognition of Companies and Legal Persons and the Protocol concerning the interpretation by the Court of Justice of the Convention of 27 September 1968 on jurisdiction and the enforcement of civil and commercial judgments, signed at Luxembourg on 3 June 1971, and to the references provided for by Article 4 of the latter Protocol.

The provisions of paragraph 1 shall apply also to references for preliminary rulings provided for by other existing or future agreements.

§ 3

In cases provided for in Article 41 of the ECSC Treaty, the text of the decision to refer the matter shall be served on the parties in the case, the Member States, the High Authority and the Special Council of Ministers.

These parties, States and institutions may, within two months from the date of such service, lodge written statements of case or written observations.

After these documents have been lodged, or where they have not been lodged within the time prescribed in the preceding subparagraph, the provisions of Article 43 *et seq.* of these rules shall apply.

Article 104
§ 1

The decisions of national courts or tribunals referred to in Article 103 of these rules shall be communicated to the Member States in the original version, accompanied by a translation into the official language of the State to which they are addressed.

§ 2

As regards the representation and attendance of the parties to the main proceedings in the preliminary ruling procedure the Court shall take account of the rules of procedure of the national court or tribunal which made the reference.

§ 3

It shall be for the national court or tribunal to decide as to the costs of the reference.

In special circumstances the Court may grant, as legal aid, assistance for the purpose of facilitating the representation or attendance of a party.

Chapter 10

SPECIAL PROCEDURES UNDER ARTICLES 103 TO 105 OF THE EURATOM TREATY

Article 105
§ 1

Four certified copies shall be lodged of an application under the third paragraph of Article 103 of the Euratom Treaty. The Commission shall be served with a copy.

§ 2

The application shall be accompanied by the draft of the agreement or contract in question, by the observations of the Commission addressed to the State concerned and by all other supporting documents.

The Commission shall submit its observations to the Court within a period of 10 days, which may be extended by the President after the State concerned has been heard.

A certified copy of the observations shall be served on that State.

§ 3

As soon as the application has been lodged the President shall designate a Judge to act as Rapporteur. The First Advocate-General shall assign the case to an Advocate-General as soon as the Judge-Rapporteur has been designated.

§ 4

The decision shall be taken in the Deliberation Room after the Advocate-General has been heard.

The agents and advisers of the State concerned and of the Commission shall be heard if they so request.

Article 106
§ 1

In cases provided for in the last paragraph of Article 104 and the last paragraph of Article 105 of the Euratom Treaty, the provisions of Articles 37 *et seq.* of these rules shall apply in a corresponding manner.

§ 2

The application shall be served on the State to which the respondent person or undertaking belongs.

Chapter 11

OPINIONS

Article 107

§ 1

A request by the Council for an Opinion under Article 228 of the EEC Treaty shall be served on the Commission. Such a request by the Commission shall be served on the Council and on the Member States. Such a request by a Member State shall be served on the Council, the Commission and the other Member States.

The President shall prescribe a period within which the institutions and Member States which have been served with a request may submit their written observations.

§ 2

The Opinion may deal not only with the question whether the envisaged agreement is compatible with the provisions of the EEC Treaty but also with the question whether the Community or any Community institution has the power to enter into that agreement.

Article 108

§ 1

As soon as the request for an Opinion has been lodged, the President shall designate a Judge to act as Rapporteur.

§ 2

The Court sitting in the Deliberation Room shall, after hearing the Advocate-General, deliver a reasoned Opinion.

§ 3

The Opinion signed by the President, by the Judges who took part in the deliberations and by the Registrar shall be served on the Council, the Commission and the Member States.

Article 109

Requests for the Opinion of the Court under the fourth paragraph of Article 95 of the ECSC Treaty shall be submitted jointly by the High Authority and the Special Council of Ministers.

The Opinion shall be delivered in accordance with the provisions of the preceding Article. It shall be communicated to the High Authority, the Special Council of Ministers and the European Parliament.

MISCELLANEOUS PROVISIONS

Article 110

§ 1

The President shall instruct any person who is required to take an oath before the Court, as witness or expert, to tell the truth or to carry out his task conscientiously and impartially, as the case may be, and shall warn him of the criminal liability provided for in his national law in the event of any breach of this duty.

§ 2

The witness shall take the oath either in accordance with the first sub-paragraph of Article 47 (5) or in the manner laid down by his national law.

Where his national law provides the opportunity to make, in judicial proceedings, a solemn affirmation equivalent to an oath as well as or instead of taking an oath, the witness may make such an affirmation under the conditions and in the form prescribed in his national law.

Where his national law provides neither for taking an oath nor for making a solemn affirmation, the procedure described in paragraph 1 shall be followed.

§ 3

Paragraph 2 shall apply *mutatis mutandis* to experts, a reference to the first sub-paragraph of Article 49 (6) replacing in this case the reference to the first subparagraph of Article 47 (5) of these Rules of Procedure.

Article 111

Subject to the provisions of Article 188 of the EEC Treaty and Article 160 of the Euratom Treaty and after consultation with the Governments concerned, the Court shall adopt supplementary rules concerning its practice in relation to:

(a) letters rogatory;

(b) applications for legal aid;

(c) reports of perjury by witnesses or experts, delivered pursuant to Article 28 of the ECSC and Euratom Statutes and Article 27 of the EEC Statute.

Article 112

These Rules replace the Rules of Procedure of the Court of Justice of the European Communities of 3 March 1959 as amended by the Decision of the Court of 11 November 1959 (OJ, 1960, p 17).

Article 113

These rules, which are authentic in the languages mentioned in Article 29 (1) of these rules, shall be published in the *Official Journal of the European Communities.*

ANNEX I

Decision on official holidays

Article 1

For the purposes of Article 80 (2) of the Rules of Procedure the following shall be official holidays:

New Year's Day;

Easter Monday;

1 May;

Ascension Day;

Whit Monday;

23 June;

24 June, where 23 June is a Sunday;

15 August;

1 November;

25 December;

26 December.

The official holidays referred to in the first paragraph hereof shall be those observed at the place where the Court of Justice has its seat.

Article 2

Article 80 (2) of the Rules of Procedure shall apply only to the official holidays mentioned in Article 1 of this Decision.

Article 3

This Decision, which shall constitute Annex I to the Rules of Procedure, shall enter into force on the same day as those rules.

It shall be published in the *Official Journal of the European Communities.*

ANNEX II

Decision on extension of time limits on account of distance

Article 1

In order to take account of distance, procedural time limits for all parties save those habitually resident in the Grand Duchy of Luxembourg shall be extended as follows:

- for the Kingdom of Belgium: two days,
- for the Federal Republic of Germany, the European territory of the French Republic and the European territory of the Kingdom of the Netherlands: six days,
- for the European territory of the Kingdom of Denmark, for the Hellenic Republic, for Ireland, for the Italian Republic, for the Kingdom of Spain, for the Portuguese Republic (with the exception of the Azores and Madeira) and for the United Kingdom: 10 days,
- for other European countries and territories: two weeks,
- for the autonomous regions of the Azores and Madeira of the Portuguese Republic: three weeks,
- for other countries, departments and territories: one month.

Article 2

This Decision, which shall constitute Annex II to the Rules of Procedure, shall enter into force on the same day as those rules.

It shall be published in the *Official Journal of the European Communities.*

Appendix IV

Rules of procedure governing appeals to the ECJ

AMENDMENTS TO THE RULES OF PROCEDURE OF THE COURT OF
JUSTICE OF THE
EUROPEAN COMMUNITIES

of 7 June 1989*

THE COURT

Having regard to Article 55 of the Protocol on the Statute of the Court of Justice of the
European Coal and Steel Community,

Having regard to the third paragraph of Article 188 of the Treaty establishing the
European Economic Community,

Having regard to the third paragraph of Article 160 of the Treaty establishing the
European Atomic Energy Community,

Whereas the establishment of a Court of First Instance of the European Communities by
Council Decision 88/591/ECSC, EEC, Euratom renders it necessary to amend the Rules
of Procedure;

With the unanimous approval of the Council given on 29 May 1989,

HAS ADOPTED THE FOLLOWING AMENDMENTS TO ITS RULES OF PROCEDURE:

Article 1

The following provisions shall be inserted after Article 109 and before the
'Miscellaneous Provisions' of the Rules of Procedure of the Court of Justice of the
European Communities adopted on 4 December 1974 (*Official Journal of the European
Communities* No L 350, 28.12.1974, p 1), and amended on 12 September 1979 (*Official
Journal of the European Communities* No L 238, 21.9.1979, p 1), 27 May 1981 (*Official
Journal of the European Communities* No L 199, 20.7.1981, p 1) and 8 May 1987
(*Official Journal of the European Communities* No L 165, 24.6.1987, p 1):

'TITLE IV

APPEALS AGAINST DECISIONS OF THE COURT OF FIRST INSTANCE OF
THE EUROPEAN COMMUNITIES

Article 110

Without prejudice to the arrangements laid down in Article 29 (2) (b) and (c) and the

---

* OJ 1989 L 241, p 1.

137

fourth sub-paragraph of Article 29 (3) of these Rules, in appeals against decisions of the Court of First Instance as referred to in Articles 49 and 50 of the Statute of the Court of Justice of the ECSC, Articles 49 and 50 of the Statute of the Court of Justice of the EEC, and Articles 50 and 51 of the Statute of the Court of Justice of the EAEC, the language of the case shall be the language of the decision of the Court of First Instance against which the appeal is brought.

Article 111

1. An appeal shall be brought by lodging an application at the Registry of the Court of Justice or of the Court of First Instance.

2. The Registry of the Court of First Instance shall immediately transmit to the Registry of the Court of Justice the papers in the case at first instance and, where necessary, the appeal.

Article 112

1. An appeal shall contain:

    (a) the name and permanent address of the party bringing the appeal, who shall be called the appellant;

    (b) the names of the other parties to the proceedings before the Court of First Instance;

    (c) the grounds on which the appeal is based and the arguments of law relied on;

    (d) the form of order sought by the appellant.

Articles 37 and 38 (2) and (3) of these Rules shall apply to appeals.

2. The decision of the Court of First Instance appealed against shall be attached to the appeal. The appeal shall state the date on which the decision appealed against was notified to the appellant.

3. If an appeal does not comply with Article 38 (2) and (3) or with paragraph 2 of this Article, Article 38 (7) of these Rules shall apply.

Article 113

1. An appeal shall seek:

    – to quash, in whole or in part, the decision of the Court of First Instance,

    – the same form of order, in whole or in part, as that sought at first instance and shall not seek a different form of order.

2. The subject-matter of the proceedings before the Court of First Instance may not be changed in the appeal.

Article 114

Notice of the appeal shall be served on all the parties to the proceedings before the Court of First Instance. Article 39 of these Rules shall apply.

Article 115

1. Any party to the proceedings before the Court of First Instance may lodge a response within two months after service on him of notice of the appeal. The time limit for lodging a response shall not be extended.

2. A response shall contain:

    (a) the name and permanent address of the party lodging it;

(b) the date on which notice of the appeal was served on him;

(c) the grounds relied on and arguments of law raised;

(d) the form of order sought.

Article 38 (2) and (3) of these Rules shall apply.

Article 116

1. A response shall seek:

- – to dismiss, in whole or in part, the appeal or to quash, in whole or in part, the decision of the Court of First Instance,

- – the same form of order, in whole or in part, as that sought at first instance and shall not seek a different form of order.

2. The subject-matter of the proceedings before the Court of First Instance may not be changed in the response.

Article 117

1. The appeal and the response may be supplemented by a reply and a rejoinder or any other pleading, where the President expressly, on application made within seven days of service of the response or of the reply, considers such further pleading necessary and expressly allows it in order to enable the party concerned to put forward its point of view or in order to provide a basis for the decision on the appeal.

2. Where in the response it is submitted that the decision of the Court of First Instance should be quashed in whole or in part on an issue which was not raised in the appeal, the appellant or any other party may submit a reply on that issue alone, within two months of the service of the response in question. Paragraph 1 shall apply to any further pleading following such a reply.

3. Where the President allows the lodging of a reply and a rejoinder, or any other pleading, he shall prescribe the period within which they are to be submitted.

Article 118

Subject to the following provisions, Articles 42 (2), 43, 44, 55 to 90, 93, 95 to 100 and 102 of these Rules shall apply to the procedure before the Court of Justice on appeal from a decision of the Court of First Instance.

Article 119

Where the appeal is, in whole or in part, clearly inadmissible or clearly unfounded, the Court may at any time, upon report of the Judge-Rapporteur and after hearing the Advocate-General, by reasoned order dismiss the appeal in whole or in part.

Article 120

1. After the submission of pleadings as provided for in Article 115 (1) and, if any, Article 117 (1) and (2) of these Rules, the Court may, upon report of the Judge-Rapporteur and after hearing the Advocate-General and the parties, decide to dispense with the oral procedure unless one of the parties objects on the ground that the written procedure did not enable him fully to defend his point of view.

2. Where, in an appeal before the Court, there is no oral procedure, the Advocate-General shall none-the-less deliver his opinion orally at a public sitting on a date to be fixed by the President.

Article 121

The report referred to in Article 44 (1) shall be presented to the Court after the pleadings provided for in Article 115 (1) and Article 117 (1) and (2) of these Rules have been lodged. The report shall contain, in addition to the recommendations provided for in Article 44 (1), a recommendation as to whether Article 120 (1) of these Rules should be applied. Where no such pleadings are lodged, the same procedure shall apply after the expiry of the period prescribed for lodging them.

Article 122

Where the appeal is unfounded or where the appeal is well founded and the Court itself gives final judgment in the case, the Court shall make a decision as to costs.

In the proceedings referred to in Article 95 (3) of these Rules:

- Article 70 of these Rules shall apply only to appeals brought by Community institutions,
- by way of derogation from Article 69 (2) of these Rules, the Court may, in appeals brought by officials or other servants of an institution, order the parties to bear all or part of their own costs where so required by equity.

If the appeal is withdrawn Article 69 (4) shall apply.

When an appeal brought by a Member State or a Community institution which did not intervene in the proceedings before the Court of First Instance is well founded, the Court of Justice may order that the parties bear their own costs or that the successful appellant pay the costs which the appeal has caused an unsuccessful party to incur.

Article 123

An application to intervene made to the Court in appeal proceedings shall be lodged before the expiry of a period of three months running from the date on which the appeal was lodged. The Court shall, after hearing the Advocate-General, give its decision in the form of an order on whether or not the intervention is allowed'.

Article 2

The former Articles 110 to 113 of the 'Miscellaneous Provisions' of these Rules shall become Articles 124 to 127 respectively.

Article 3

These amendments to the Rules of Procedure, which are authentic in the languages mentioned in Article 29 (1) of the Rules of Procedure, shall be published in the *Official Journal of the European Communities* and shall enter into force on the day after the date of their publication.

Index